Introduction

Years ago I was confronted by a Calvinist about my belief that God loves and wants to save everyone. He stated that Adam *had* to sin; that he had no alternative. He also said Christ only provided salvation for some, and had them picked out before creation. They had no choice in the matter, as man has no truly free will. He quoted some Bible passages, especially Romans 9. I had never investigated Calvinism to any degree. I was uneasy, wondering if I was wrong; that maybe what he said was true. If it was, I knew I would have to embrace it, as horrible as it was. That started a journey of years, in which I read both Calvinist and opposing opinions, and did much personal Bible study to come to a final conclusion.

John Piper, a noted Calvinist, states in a YouTube video that, in his experience, the freewill camp's main refutation of Calvinism is simply that it is horrible and unthinkable. It is not the biblically strong view that Calvinism is. I find that shocking and humorous. I concluded exactly the opposite; that the freewill view, apart from anyone's feelings, is not just stronger, but immeasurably stronger—mountain-to-mole-hill stronger. The Calvinist view has some *apparent* biblical support, but it is very weak overall with impossible contradictions. I see them doing a disturbing amount of redefining and word gymnastics to support it. Do we all engage in some *fitting together* when formulating our biblical systems? Of course; we have no choice. But when it becomes extreme, it loses credibility. Many have come out of Calvinism because of a recognition that too many things didn't add up.

I am convinced that arriving at this doctrine with logical, independent study, free from the specific influence of one of its teachers borders on the impossible, which may be a reason it is a relative latecomer in Christian church history. I see it, as do many thousands of others, as man-made. Many have said it turns God into a monster; and I have to agree.

Because I saw in Calvinism a source of much potential damage, not the least of which is to the true God's glory, I felt compelled to undertake a written refutation of certain parts of it. Many Christians suffer in Calvinist churches, and need to know this view is not the only one.

I was raised in a Christian home, received a ministerial bachelor's degree from Tennessee Temple University, and have served all my life in various church ministries and missions. I am also a college math professor, having done my graduate work at Texas Tech. I believe logic is important in biblical interpretation. The Holy Spirit will not bring us to illogical conclusions. He *is* ultimate logic. Hermeneutical training is rooted in finding sound and reasonable interpretations. There is no better training in logic than rigorous mathematical exercises and proofs. Math is, in fact, more about logic than numbers. Although biblical interpretation does not always lend itself to the same precise, unbendable conclusions as those in mathematics, I have striven to implement this same sense of precision and rigor in my own analysis of this doctrine. That said, I claim nothing about myself as a reason why you should listen to me. I only present the Scriptures. Truth is truth, whether presented by a twelve-year-old kid or a doctorated seminary professor. I leave it to you to read and to make your own determination.

I do not entertain the hope that a firmly entrenched Calvinist's mind will be changed from reading this. That is unlikely. My hope is simply that it may benefit someone who is seeking.

Kevin Williamson

Did God Provide Salvation for All People?

This treatise will examine some of the biblical difficulties of Calvinism, a doctrine espoused by the reformer John Calvin, which ultimately negates man's ability to make right choices, and uses the fact of God's sovereignty to assert that only God's will is ever exercised in anything that comes to pass, including salvation.

Before I begin, I want to stress that I believe there are good people in Calvinism that love God and are dedicated to His service. I have had friendships with them. We believe in the same Jesus and the same Cross as the basis for redemption. They are my brothers and sisters in Christ. They truly believe they have used the Bible correctly in arriving at their conclusions and are not without their proof texts. They also tenaciously and admirably defend the glory and sovereignty of God in their own way.

If you are of Calvinistic persuasion, please know that nothing in this book is intended to insult or to offend in any way, although I forewarn that I will speak frankly and in no uncertain terms. I believe direct talk is warranted; and I won't be dancing delicately around the issue. I believe this is a case where good people have subscribed to a heretical doctrine; and I plan to make that case. I have chosen an informal style, somewhat more like a living room conversation, over the style of a formal textbook, in which I sometimes "poke fun" or use some strong wordings. But I mean it with regard to the doctrine; not the integrity, character, or intelligence of its adherents.

Regarding designations, if you object to the term "Calvinist," the fact is, I'm not quite sure what other term is better. I don't particularly favor it, but have utilized it because, in my experience, it is the prevailing designation. It is nothing more than a tool with which to refer to the doctrine or its adherents, many of whom refer to themselves as such. The view I support has been around since the Church Fathers. Some might call me an Arminian, but I don't, since Arminius doesn't go back more than a few hundred years; and I don't necessarily agree with all his writings. I mostly just refer to myself and others of like thought as being in the free will camp. I even sometimes humorously refer to us as freewillers. Some call us traditionalists, and I consider this fitting also.

I have done my best to research carefully the Calvinist belief system. I will not knowingly misquote, distort, or incorrectly describe it. A layer of difficulty is added by the fact that there are different flavors of the doctrine as with any system. I have done my best to be precise in my portrayals and fair with my arguments.

It is helpful to point out that the controversy can be concisely reduced to a fundamental question. *How is the sovereignty of God defined?* Calvinists believe man has no truly free will. God alone decides, decrees, and brings about everything that happens, including our sins. The traditional view, my view, says man has free will, and can do things that God does not wish and never intended. However, in His sovereignty, He sets the parameters that limit how far man can go; and He will fulfill His purposes regardless of what man does. This was the view of the Church Fathers for almost 400 years until Augustine espoused the *determinist* view, which Calvin made popular many hundreds of years later.

Frankly, I recommend that information be obtained from both Calvinist and freewill sources. That way I am not your sole representation on Calvinist beliefs. Besides, I am a big believer in examining all sides of any issue. That is a big part of independent thinking, which I have always strongly encouraged. Many have allowed a preacher, a mentor, family members, or some other person to form their doctrine for them. I urge you, reader, to do your own study, pray for guidance, and form your own belief system. This requires a lot of work though, and sadly, some are not willing to put forth the effort to truly be students and disciples of the Word.

The purpose of this work is to focus mostly on certain sub points, rather than to give a comprehensive treatise on biblical election. I don't believe it is possible this side of eternity to perfectly explain how God's sovereignty and man's free will work together. But there are smaller points which I believe can be addressed with a very high degree of certainty; and most of the emphasis will be on these. They will be made with the ultimate aim of refuting three major positions of Calvinist doctrine, which are the natural corollaries of their definition of sovereignty, namely:

1. **Unconditional Election** - God alone chooses the eternal destinies of all persons. They are fixed and unchangeable.
2. **Limited Atonement** - Jesus died only for those He chose to save, the elect.
3. **Irresistible Grace** - God's saving grace cannot be rejected by man. If He wants to save someone, He essentially does so by force.

They are the ULI of TULIP, the common acronym used to conveniently list the five main tenets of Calvinism. I will not be dwelling on *Total Depravity* or *Perseverance of the Saints*, the T and P of TULIP, as I don't consider these to contribute to the damage that results from Calvinism.

These ULI tenets stand or fall on the definition of God's sovereignty. If He is the only one making decisions, they are necessary. If man has free will, and God is not the only one making decisions, they collapse. It is important to read and study with this big picture in mind. Notice that they depend on each other. Unconditional election leads naturally to Christ dying only for the elect; and if God is the only one choosing, irresistible grace is a necessary conclusion.

If you speak with Calvinists and read their books, you will soon see that they perceive God's creation as one in which He purposely engineered two groups of humans: one accepted and blessed, and the other rejected and ultimately tormented. One Calvinist friend of mine even told me God's plan is for these two groups to exist so that the accepted ones will feel extremely blessed and special upon seeing the contrasting fate of the rejected ones.

(Let me inject that I will often word a Calvinist belief in a way they would never do to reflect the ugly reality of it. Parts of this belief system are truly horrible. It is understandable that they would try to put the best possible face on it.)

So, Calvinists believe that God, in His sovereignty, decreed and *ensured* that the devil and Adam *would fall*. They were not allowed to obey, but would be blamed and judged for disobeying anyway. Humanity would then need to be saved. A relative few pre-selected ones, the elect, are forgiven and saved, leaving the larger group of unloved and rejected humanity hopeless and damned to eternal torment.

An overarching belief of Calvinism is that the *sole reason* God ever does anything is *for His own glory*. In my opinion, no accuracy is lost by describing the Calvinist God's plan as His pushing us off a cliff so He could save a few and get glory. I am also at a complete loss as to how putting someone in danger just so you can save them, just so you can get glory, makes you deserving of *any* glory; not to mention the fact that no one who does things only to look like a hero is *ever* thought of as a hero. Heroes get glory simply by being who they are. *That* determines what they do.

I maintain God *cannot help* but be glorified just by being who He is. He doesn't have to plan and pursue it. What He does follows from *His nature*, not contrivances. I am not denying there are times in the Bible where God displayed His power to glorify Himself; but, to say the Cross was solely the pursuit of glory destroys the beauty of it. What a terrible insult to Christ! He did not sit in Heaven and think, "How good will I look and what great glory will I gain if I act the part of a hero and sacrifice myself as if my motives were *only* love and compassion for man." As one critic put it, that is more about Christ loving Himself than His creatures. The fact is, the Cross was *pure love and compassion in action*. It stemmed from the *nature* of God. Glory could not help but follow from the realization that the motives were truly these, in all their unadulterated purity.

In fact, judging from Romans 9, where Paul was willing to permanently sacrifice himself in hell for Israel, the case could be made that Jesus loves us *more than* Himself; unless of course, you maintain that Paul had a greater love than God. Calvinists actually believe he did though! They say God does not share these feelings! Why did God have Paul put this in His Word then?—to show that His love is not as strong as a man's?

I think many will also see that if you follow their ideas to their natural ends, you will be forced to conclude that God's concern with man making right choices as well as His anger against sin, is essentially a show. They will not say it like this. But they do teach that God *wanted* sin to exist, He made sure it would happen, and man's choices are actually inconsequential. Only God Himself truly makes any real choices, from whether we are saved or not to *every sin we commit*. To say anything else is to damage the fact of God's absolute sovereignty. If we say man has a truly free will, we reduce God to a beggar, pitifully pleading for man to please, please accept Him. They emphasize God is a King. He alone decides who will be saved.

Again, don't take my word on Calvinist doctrine. You can investigate and verify for yourself. There are many books, online documents, and YouTube videos on the subject. Let's weigh this doctrine on the Bible scale, keeping in mind the aforementioned three positions of theirs.

First, let me point out how the material is organized. I have not dealt with each tenet separately. Rather, I have made *twelve claims*. Each claim targets one or more of the tenets and/or the definition of God's sovereignty they rest on. I give many biblical passages for you to consider. Please take time to look up and read them. I ask you to decide for yourself if these claims are truly biblical, or if I have misused the Bible. I also ask you to keep the terms *unconditional election, limited atonement,* and *irresistible grace* mentally highlighted as you read. After the claims have been presented, we will look at some of the typical objections and proof texts of Calvinists. At the very end you will find a brief topical list of passages against each of the three tenets that you might find helpful.

I want to point out that I am a big believer in using logic in approaching the Bible. By this I mean simply using sound reasoning to arrive at truth. For anyone who says we should rely on the Holy Spirit, not man's reasoning, I do not disagree. But, the Holy Spirit guides us *only* into the logic, or truth, of His Word. God *is* ultimate logic. He gave us a brain with reasoning powers that is programmed for logical thought, with which we communicate with Him and each other. True, we need to ask the Holy Spirit's guidance to correctly reason and interpret, but it does not mean that after doing so, we throw logic out the window and believe whatever we want. If we do, there will be a serious problem. I've seen too many Christians treat the Bible like a magic book. Whatever they *feel* it is saying, or *want* it to say, becomes fact, not what it is *actually* saying. But, words *mean what they mean*, and *only* what they mean, completely apart from our feelings or desires.

One further note: I grew up with the King James Bible and have continued with it all my life out of habit. It does have some archaic uses of language; for instance, "all men" when it means all people. We know, of course, that both genders are equally important to God. Please understand this, and don't take offense at a supposed diminishing of the female sex when the KJV is quoted. I also use "man" to mean humans in general, per the long-standing but somewhat fading convention. Again, I believe, men, women, and children are all of equal importance and significance.

Here I will present the following twelve claims with accompanying scriptures:

1. Although God is absolutely sovereign, this does not mean He forced sin into existence because it was His will.

2. God's will is constantly obstructed by man. He grieves over not being able to bless and save the rebellious.

3. God uses pleas based on reason, not force, to urge man to repent.

4. God loves everyone, and desires to save them.

5. Jesus was heartbroken at not being able to save everyone.

6. The Bible is full of warnings about making the right choices.

7. Evangelism and testimony make a genuine difference in eternal destinies.

8. The unpardonable sin makes impossible the position that each person's destiny is fixed and unchangeable.

9. Calvinism makes Satan completely irrelevant.

10. Calvinism makes it impossible to make sense of the biblical teaching that we were children of wrath and on our way to Hell before being saved.

11. If Calvinism is biblically sound, there will be no regrets for people in Hell.

12. Calvinism makes the Judgment Seat of Christ meaningless.

1. *Although God is absolutely sovereign, this does not mean He forced sin into existence because it was His will*.

The Baptist Confession of Faith of 1689, a Calvinistic document, says, "God hath decreed in himself, from all eternity, by the most wise and holy counsel of his own will, freely and unchangeably, all things, whatsoever comes to pass; yet so as thereby is God neither the author of sin nor hath fellowship with any therein…"

It further states, "Man, in his state of innocency, had freedom and power to will and to do that which was good and well-pleasing to God, *but yet was unstable*, so that he might fall from it." (italics added)

Let's look at the first claim. It seems to contain an inherent contradiction. On the one hand, *nothing* happens that God did not specifically will and decree. However, when the obvious question of the origin and source of evil arises, the authors seem to realize their doctrine inevitably makes God the author of sin. How do they overcome this problem?—simply by stating that He is not! Problem solved.

What of the second claim? How do they separate God from Adam's sin in light of this doctrine? They call Adam "unstable." They avoid calling him "sinful" in his original state, so that God will not be the author of sin. He was simply created unstable (on purpose) so that God's will for him to sin *would* be carried out. That way, in their minds, God could *indirectly* force disobedience to take place, but avoid a *direct* connection. How does this strike you? Does it not smack of a ridiculous attempt to have it both ways? God forced disobedience to take place. He decreed that it *would* happen. He *made sure* man would be powerless to obey. But God is not responsible for the disobedience it in any way! This senseless mumbo jumbo is the foundation of Calvinism. By the way, how could Adam have an instability that makes him fall, but at the same time have "freedom and power" to do right? What strange double talk! It can only be one or the other.

Apparently, God employed similarly defective workmanship in order to induce Satan to sin as well! I ask, does this sound biblical to you? Is this truly the God of whom the cherubim in Isaiah 6 continually cry, "Holy, holy, holy, is the Lord of hosts; the whole earth is full of His glory"?

I submit this does not stack up biblically or logically. The fact is, regardless of how much they try to deny it, this doctrine makes God the first cause of evil—by design; truly the author of sin. There simply is no other conclusion unless we abandon all common sense. You have to answer this question. How does the Creator force sin to happen without being the agent of evil? The document founders wrestled with this. They knew it meant something bad would have to be in Adam, and they would need to try to separate God from it.

Let's look closer at this supposed *instability*. For one thing, what does it mean? They give no definition. Secondly, where does the Bible *ever* say anything like this? Nowhere! You will search cover-to-cover in vain. It is purely an invention of man to try to get them out of a very awkward problem. The funny thing is, it fixes nothing at all. Just visualize it. God wants to create man and *make sure he sins* without being the author of evil. If He gives truly free will, it could go either way. He can't allow the possibility that Adam chooses right. How does He force sin to happen? There has to be something *in Adam* that will *make* him do it. So they name this thing "instability." I find it very telling and humorous that they say he "*was* unstable" rather than that he "*was made* unstable." So how exactly did God get this instability into Adam without doing it himself and thereby being responsible? That's the problem. By definition, it must be a *bent toward evil* or it wouldn't make him choose evil. So let's call it what it is: an *irresistible compulsion to do evil*. It couldn't have come from Adam. He didn't create *himself*. Did it just sort of happen randomly apart from God's doing? No, God was the *only* agent in the origin of every one of Adam's components. Even Calvinists have to agree with this by their definition of sovereignty. *Nothing* has *ever* happened, or *can ever* happen but what God specifically willed, designed, decreed, and brought about.

If you follow the trail of logic dictated by their own words, it leaves only one possible conclusion. This instability, AKA a compulsion toward evil, was *built* into Adam by God! The Calvinist God **made** Adam evil! There is no way to reason that away. The instability clause solves nothing. They tried to slip an excuse for God in sideways and ignore the implications, but it simply doesn't work. And now, the *Fall* is a meaningless term. Adam was *created* fallen. I've even read Calvinists who explicitly say that man, left alone even before the Fall (whatever that means at this point), would have naturally tended toward evil apart from an intervention by God. That parallels this document's claims. What they don't want to highlight is that the only one who could possibly be responsible for that is God.

What about Satan and the fallen angels? The same thing applies. God supposedly decided a select number of angels would be evil. *He wanted them to disobey so He would have something to get "angry" about!* How did He force that to happen? Again, it could not be random by this theology. He had to implant a compulsion to evil in every one of them to eliminate the chance they might choose right. That is a lot of evil surgeries by a God who supposedly hates sin. Were they given the option to do right? Were they given the choice whether to be evil or not. No, they weren't! I would ask what kind of creator puts evil in His beings so they will rebel, and then blames them and burns them. What a sick and twisted "justice." I have to agree with Dr. Leighton Flowers, a former Calvinist, that when a being acts devilish, it is because he *is* devilish. How Calvinists can call their version of God "good" or "loving" is beyond me. Many have a sense that something is wrong but believe they must concur. They have a hard time saying it with conviction or feeling though.

Non-Calvinists read the Bible and know that a holy God could not force disobedience. If He participated, he would no longer be who He is. (I Pet. 1:15,16) In order for this to be true, man had to be completely responsible for it in every conceivable way. This requires a truly free will, completely and totally independent of that of the Creator, in which Adam and Satan *could have chosen to do right* as well as wrong. The Bible refutes this idea that Adam was somehow defective, unstable, or evil, and teaches he was good and upright as originally created. (Gen. 1:31; Ecc. 7:29) It says God saw that *everything* He made was *very good*. Was there instability in the sun? No. Was there instability in the animals? No. Was the moon wobbling, partially out of control? No. Were there defective atomic elements? Was there instability in the ocean? Was gravity occasional cutting out? No. Was there instability in Adam? Calvinists say yes. He came out of the oven half-baked. God had to make him defective, pre-disposed to sin, so his failure of the test would be certain. I submit this is an invention of man, a straight-out lie from the devil.

Furthermore, James 1:13,14 says God never tempts man. In this context, it means He won't push us toward evil or entice us, exactly like Calvinists say He *did*. He allowed Satan to enter the garden and tempt them. He didn't send him. Adam and Eve made their *own* choices, not God.

If the Creator forced disobedience on Adam, passages like that in James are a farce. The idea that God preordains and brings about sin, but is not responsible for it is a *fatal contradiction* to anyone who cares about the meaning of words, logic, and common sense. Some resort to simply calling it a mystery that we cannot understand. I have to agree that is certainly the best way to justify hanging onto a pet contradiction. Just call it a mystery! It gets you out of the unenviable task of trying to explain it in a way that doesn't sound insane. The fact is, however, that there is a big difference between a contradiction, which is self-cancelling, and a mystery, which is something difficult to understand.

John MacArthur uses this just-call-it-a-mystery technique. I've seen him do it. He uses circular reasoning, assuming what he wants to defend as the proof that it is true. Here's how it works:

Step One: Assume and state the Calvinist position to be indisputably biblical.
Step Two: When asked to explain the blatant contradictions, say, "I can't. I'm not God."
Step Three: Say, "We've already seen it's what the Bible

says, so we have to accept it no matter what."

It's perfect. This way you can claim anything you want and you don't have to debate, explain, or prove anything! Some, however, actually attempt forays into this mess. Calvinist David Mathis, in his book "The Doctrine of God" in chapter 9 maintains that, although God brings sin about, He is blameless. He speaks of the difficulty of putting this into words. I have placed his comments in bold face.

> **"Therefore, there has been much discussion among theologians as to what verb should best describe God's agency in regard to evil. Some initial possibilities: authors, brings about, causes, controls, creates, decrees, foreordains, incites, includes within his plan, makes happen, ordains, permits, plans, predestines, predetermines, produces, stands behind, wills. Many of these are extra-scriptural terms; none of them are perfectly easy to define in this context. So theologians need to give some careful thought about which of these terms, if any, should be affirmed, and in what sense. Words are the theologian's tools. In a situation like this, none of the possibilities is fully adequate. There are various advantages and disadvantages among the different terms. Let us consider some of those that are most frequently discussed."**

In my experience, this problem with hunting for the right words is common when trying to state a contradiction so that is does not seem to contradict. *None* of them work very well! He then tries to answer the question whether God is the "author" of sin.

"The term author is almost universally condemned in the theological literature. It is rarely defined, but it seems to mean both that God is the efficient cause of evil and that by causing evil he actually does something wrong."

Based on what he says next, he seems to be making the distinction that if by "author," we mean that God causes evil, and *thereby He is doing something wrong*, then He is not the author of evil. But if we conclude He is doing nothing wrong by bringing evil about, then He can be considered the author. Sorry, but that's not how definitions work! An instigator is an instigator regardless of any other factors.

"And as we saw [in chapter 4] God does bring about sinful human actions. To deny this, or to charge God with wickedness on account of it, is not open to a Bible-believing Christian. Somehow, we must confess both that God has a role in bringing evil about, and that in doing so he is holy and blameless. . . . God does bring sins about, but always for his own good purposes. So in bringing sin to pass he does not himself commit sin.

I can only respond with a stunned, "What?!" Is he kidding?! God is righteous in causing evil because He does it for His own good purposes?! If that is the criterion, He can lie, deceive, torture the innocent, build compulsions to sin into man, or commit any evil you want to name, and He is still holy and blameless. It seems what he's saying at the root is that God can do anything He wants, good or evil; but for Him, evil isn't evil. One wonders at this point if the words *holy* and *pure* have <u>any meaning at all</u> when applied to God!

What is the Bible saying when it tells us He is holy? The fact is, holiness means *staying away from the unholy*. That means there are bounds! Is the definition different for God? No! I Peter 1:16 is clear that God holds Himself to the same standard. He tells us to be holy as *He is holy*. So, He *avoids* the unholy just as He commands us to do! The definition is *not different* for Him. He is bounded! Is it wrong for us to lie? Of course. Numbers 23:19 says He will not lie. Is it evil for us to not love our enemies and not seek their good? Then it would be evil, and inconsistent with His nature, not to truly love His enemies and seek their good. Is it evil for me to manipulate someone else into doing evil? Then it is evil for God to do so, by His *own criterion*. Is it evil and unjust to blame and punish someone for doing something you forced them into doing? Neither will the righteous Judge of the earth do so.

I John 2:6, speaking of Jesus says, "He that saith he abideth in him ought himself also to walk, even as he walked." So Jesus is our example. WWJD "What would Jesus do?" Jesus is God; and if I am to follow the example of the Calvinist God, then I'm not doing evil when I push others into sin. But, clearly that is a false statement; and it is anti-biblical and foolish to declare that evil is just fine for God! (Obviously there are things under God's purview but not under ours. God decides when people die. That would be murder for us except under certain circumstances.)

John Piper, perhaps the most influential Calvinist in the United States, preaches that God determines and brings about every evil thing you will ever think or do. *He chooses what you will choose*. You *have* to do it. Yet He is absolutely holy and blameless, and it is *your fault alone!* You can read and hear Piper on his website www.desiringgod.org. He claims there is no contradiction, and actually tries to explain how this can be true. I find his words to be gibberish and nonsensical.

It aptly demonstrates that a person can believe anything in the world and will cling to that belief in the face of logic or any evidence to the contrary. In fact, he "knows" he is right. There are people today, intelligent people, who truly believe the earth is flat. They can articulate why they believe that, and even make fun of those who believe in the "hoax" of the moon landings and a spherical earth. They have websites, blogs, and even a flat earthers dating site! Of course, *both* groups cannot be right. One is dead wrong, and the other is not. The same applies to the Calvinist view and the freewill view. One is a categorically false doctrine, and the remaining one is right. The big question is, which is which? You know where I stand. I maintain that the *overwhelming* weight of evidence is on the free will (traditional) side. It is what was generally believed until Calvin, and is still the view of the *vast* majority of Christendom. By the way, if Calvinists are right, that means God decreed that most of His own children would reject the true doctrine of salvation, namely, unconditional election. Doesn't that seem very strange?

If God did not bring about Adam's sin, then the Fall was the result of man's free will, not some mythical decree of God you can't find in the Bible. If so, the Calvinist definition of God's sovereignty is false; and therefore, the doctrines of *unconditional election, limited atonement,* and *irresistible grace* fall with it. They only make sense if God alone determines everything that happens.

I feel I could have stopped here. I would conclusively reject Calvinism as heresy based only on what we've seen so far. But there's more—a lot more. Let's look at some other evidences that man has a free will.

2. *God's will is constantly obstructed by man. He grieves over not being able to bless and save the rebellious.*

It is biblically clear that, although God knew from

the beginning that sin would occur and made provision for it, it grieves Him deeply because of His holy nature. (Gen. 6:6,7; Isa. 63:8-10; Eph. 4:30) It could never be His will to bring it about. It would be ridiculous to say He is deeply disturbed over something he made happen! The fact is man makes choices God never intended him to make.

In Numbers 13 and 14, the people refused to enter the Promised Land for fear of the inhabitants. God's sovereignty, by Calvinist definition, means He willed and planned their disobedience. Read this for yourself and see if it makes any sense to say He *wanted* them to rebel. He was so angry He would have destroyed the people but for the intercession of Moses.

One of the tenets of Calvinism is *irresistible grace.* It states that when the Holy Spirit wants to have mercy on an individual, and deals with his or her heart, that person *has to* respond positively, as the Spirit's grace cannot be rejected. In other words, God forces people to make right choices; meaning they themselves make no actual choice. The only reason some are not saved is because they are not chosen, or predestinated, to salvation; so the Spirit never even makes grace available to them. But it is abundantly demonstrated, not in a few ambiguous verses, but in *numerous* places in Scripture that this is not true. God sincerely desires to bless and save people, and is grieved when they will not allow Him to.

In Ezekiel 18:30-32 and 33:11, God pleads with Israel to turn to Him. He says, "I have no pleasure in the death of the wicked; but that the wicked turn from his way and live: turn ye, turn ye from your evil ways; for why will ye die, O house of Israel?" In other words, it was not necessary for them to be destroyed. It could not be clearer that this was not God's will. But it happened anyway. He asks why they are going to die. If He had predestinated them to Hell with no hope of salvation, this question would have been the *height* of absurdity. The answer would be that they never had another alternative!

Deuteronomy 5:29 says, "O that there were such an heart in them, that they would fear me, and keep all my commandments always, that it might be well with them, and with their children forever!" God clearly yearns to bless Israel, but because of man's free will, He was compelled to partially destroy them.

In Deuteronomy 32:29 God says, "O that they were wise, that they understood this, that they would consider their latter end!" Why wish longingly for something you can easily make happen?

In Isaiah 5:1-7 God compares His beloved Israel to a vineyard, to which He did everything possible to make productive. He then "looked that it should bring forth grapes, and it brought forth wild [inferior] grapes." He yearned for Israel to be obedient. He **looked for it**, but it didn't happen. Why? Because man has a truly free will. He is not created a puppet. Other passages that make this very clear are Isaiah 48:17-19; 65:2-7; and Psalm 81:8-16. Try to read these passages and inject the God of Calvinism into them, a God who willed everything He is protesting; a God who *wanted* that rebellion to happen; who *chose* and *decreed* it would happen. Nothing could be more baseless, irrational, and contradictory. He was broken-hearted. He tells how He would have blessed them if they had only listened to Him. But, according to this heresy, *their rebellion was **never** the obstacle*. The obstacle was *God Himself*, who didn't allow them to choose right. These were His *chosen* people!

Jeremiah 32:35 **alone** destroys the doctrine of Calvinism. God says, "They built the high places of Baal in the Valley of the Son of Hinnom, to offer up their sons and daughters to Molech, though I did not command them, **nor did it enter into my mind**, that they should do this abomination, to cause Judah to sin." Calvinists say God predetermined their actions before the foundation of the world. I ask you, "How did He predetermine and ordain this if it *never entered His mind*?" This doctrine is foolishness.

Piper says all evildoing comes from God. He is the cause. But I John 2:16 says, "For all that is in the world, the lust of the flesh, and the lust of the eyes, and the pride of life, **is not of the Father**, but is of the world."

In Ezekiel 22:24-31, God sought for a man to intercede for wicked Israel so as not to destroy her. Because he found no one, His judgment fell. Calvinists would simply say it was not God's will to find an intercessor, but this is not what an honest reading reveals. When God says, "I sought for a man," He means us to take Him at His word! He *wanted* someone to intercede, but there was no one available. *God doesn't use His sovereignty to eliminate our capacity to choose.* Man can and does resist God and His grace. (Gen. 6:3-6; Jn. 5:40; Mat. 23:37; Eze. 33:7,8,11) Man has a free will!

Genesis 6:3 tells us God's Spirit **strives** with man. What a strange statement if He simply makes His will happen with a thought. In verse six, He was *sorry* He had made man. How could that happen if He is simply unfolding the plan He *always had*?! Did the Calvinist God not think His decrees through? I Thessalonians 5:19 teaches that the Spirit can be quenched. Ephesians 4:30 says the Spirit is often **grieved**. How can this be true if He is the only one deciding who will do what? *Calvinism makes God constantly at odds with Himself.* The doctrine of *irresistible grace* is overwhelmingly and easily demonstrated to be in error if we just listen to Scripture without an agenda. The only reason it was ever propounded in the first place was that it is a necessary corollary to the supposed absence of free will. The two are, to a large degree, the same teaching.

Think about one last contradiction while we are on the subject of God's will. Jesus taught in the Lord's Prayer to ask, "Thy will be done." Why would Jesus instruct us to request that of God when the **foundation** of Calvinism is that *nothing except God's will can or will ever be done*?! What a useless and ridiculous request! You might as well pray, "Father, please keep being God," or "Please bring prophecy to pass." But the teaching makes perfect sense if God allows His will to be violated at times by man, and His children pray that less of that would happen.

3. *God uses pleas based on reason, not force, to urge man to repent.*

In Isaiah 1:16-20, He says, "Let us reason together." He then presents arguments to Israel, urging them to repent. He pleads and makes His case with them in Isaiah 43:25-28 and Micah 6:1-5. If God's system is simply to snap His fingers, change their hearts, and *make* them repent, what is the point of reasoning? How does *unconditional election* and *irresistible grace* make sense here? Why would I argue with someone if I could just control their mind and decide they would agree with everything I said?

Another of many examples that God does not manipulate minds is Exodus 13:17,18 where He chose a route for the exodus of Israel that would not expose them to the Philistines so that they would not immediately be engaged in battle, get discouraged, and return to Egypt. Could He not easily have altered their thinking in an instant so that war would not scare them? But He doesn't do that, at least not as His general modus operandi. He has given man a will of his own.

4. *God loves everyone, and desires to save them.*

Mat. 7:13,14 is one of the saddest passages in the Bible. It shows that only a small fraction of humanity will be saved. Calvinists say that God *unconditionally elected* the destinies of each person before the foundation of the world. He alone chose, not because of anything in them, but because He simply wanted it to be so. They had nothing to do with it. But, Lamentations 3:33 says God does not *willingly* afflict man. That means it is not His <u>will</u> for people to go to Hell! How does His predestination to Hell of **most** people before they were ever born, so that they can be horribly and eternally afflicted *not contradict* this passage? I see no greater contradiction in the statement that Hitler was a loving guy!

Calvinists I've read try to say it simply means He feels negatively that His plan requires Him to do this to people to accomplish His goals. In other words, He is not actually giving them the option of being saved. He is going to burn them alive because He wants to, but He feels kind of bad about it, and this shows His "goodness."

Some Calvinists say God has at least two wills; one with which He feels a desire to save the reprobate, and another, His decretal will, in which for His purposes, He wishes to damn them. So what they are effectively saying is that He would like to save them, but not as much as He would like not to save them. If that's true, how could anyone possibly infer that God is loving and merciful? Calvinists insist He is because they have no choice. Are you convinced?

On the other hand, if Lamentations is highlighting His *genuine* invitation to save them if they will submit, it is one of the most important and relevant statements in the Bible. It is *vital* to the message of the Gospel. Ezekiel 18:23 says, "Have I any pleasure at all that the wicked should die? saith the Lord GOD: and not that he <u>should return from his ways, and live</u>?" Oh, so the wicked person that died in his sin didn't have to? He had the option of returning from his wickedness and being saved? It says so right here. But Calvinists don't believe it.

One of their main tenets states that *Christ died and provided salvation only for the elect* (limited atonement).

Most of the world has no recourse for even being saved! There is no penalty paid for their sin! They were *born* to go to Hell. This torture of people who were given no option to choose righteousness is for the express purpose of getting God glory.

I find that astonishing; and would ask how that could bring him glory in any way. That would be the very definition of a monster when thinking of any other being, as I'm sure Calvinists would agree. But logic is abandoned, and definitions are magically altered and refitted when the subject is God. Goodness, love, and justice must take on *much more restricted meanings*. In fact, they become completely unrecognizable. The argument is, God needed to show His wrath against evil, so He couldn't save everyone. I would ask, *"Didn't the Cross show that better than anything else ever could have!?"* He could have saved everyone and have *still* shown His wrath. Why did the God *who is love* choose not to save everyone when He could have? Nothing would be left out to complete His plan; except of course, billions and billions of people on fire screaming for all eternity with no hope.

R. C. Sproul, a very prominent Calvinist author could not answer this question. He says in his book, "Chosen By God" page 35, "The only answer I can give to this question is that I don't know. I have no idea why God saves some but not all. I don't doubt for a moment that God has the power to save all, but I know that he does not choose to save all. I don't know why. . . ."

As I see it, that is a *huge* problem for this doctrine. Of course, if the opposite view is true, and Hell is the just result of the wicked choosing evil when they could have chosen Jesus, then God will be *truly* glorified as *real* justice, not the Calvinist *fake* justice, is served.

Did God really provide salvation only for the elect? Let's see. He reveals Himself as a God of infinite love. In Micah 7:18, He *delights* in mercy. This mercy is base on a pure *agape* love which we cannot fully comprehend. Furthermore, He doesn't just love, He IS love. (I John 4:7) It is His essence, His very core!

It is, therefore, very important to understand the definition of biblical love, the love of which God consists, in order to understand what He is saying about Himself. Is this love a feeling, an emotion? Certainly there is such a thing as a loving feeling, but that is not what is spoken of here. God loved the *world*, His enemies. Jesus cried out even at the cross, "Father forgive them, for they know not what they do." Because He loved the world, He *gave*; that is, He did what was necessary to seek their well-being. We were not lovable. We were not attractive. We did not evoke warm, fuzzy emotions in God. We were repugnant, dirty, sinful. But biblical agape love is not a feeling. It is a *choice*. It is a decision to seek the well-being of another regardless of how they make us feel (unconditional love). It is an *action*, not an emotion. It is impossible to claim you love someone with agape love in the absence of a decision to seek their well-being.

God commands us to have this love for our neighbor, without distinction (Matthew 22:39) We are even commanded to love our enemies (Matthew 5:44). Is this an emotional love? Are we commanded to "feel" something for them? Of course not. We can't decide our emotions. But we can choose to do what we don't feel like doing, and *seek their good*.

This understanding of biblical love forces many Calvinists to conclude that <u>God does not love all people,</u> because if He did, He would seek their good. But I would ask you how the God who IS love turns it on and off. "I'll save that one, not that one, not that one, not that one. I'll take that one, not that one, etc." Besides this, the Bible teaches that God loves, protects, and even assigns angels to *all children*. (Matthew 18:5,6,10) Does that mean they start out as elect, and at some point, most of them lose their election? Or maybe God *temporarily* has a loving feeling for those whom He has already predestinated to Hell, then it wears off! After all, they are cute when they're children!

Think about it! How could God describe to us how much He loves children if, rather than actually seek their well-being, He has already condemned most of them to Hell without ever giving the vast majority of them the option of being saved?

The Bible teaches, however, that God loves and wants to save everyone. Please consider an impossible contradiction when the command for us to love all men is considered through the eyes of a Calvinist. You will notice that all attributes that God commands His children to have and practice: holiness, love, purity, righteousness, wisdom, humility, servitude, etc., are things in which He has always surpassed us. He has and does all of these things Himself, but to an infinitely greater degree without exception. Even the King of Kings and Lord of Lords proved Himself to be the greatest Servant there has ever been.

Now if He commands us to love <u>all people</u>, even our enemies, <u>will He Himself do less?</u> Is He a hypocrite? There is no way. Matt 5:44, 45 says that in loving our enemies, we will be the children of our heavenly Father. What does that mean? It means like Father like son. God is telling us to do **what He does**! We are to follow Him in love.

I John 2:6 says we are to walk as Christ would. He is our example. He will love His enemies with a deeper love than we *ever* could. In fact the only way Christ could be our sacrifice was if He fulfilled the Law for us. In Matthew 22:37-40, He says all the law is fulfilled in keeping two commandments. These are that we love God with all our heart, and that we *love our neighbor as ourselves*. Who is our neighbor? Is it just our favorites? No. Everyone loves their favorites! It is everyone around us.

Jesus loved everyone around Him, which would have included His enemies and those that would never repent!

What is the source of this love with which He has commanded *us* to love all people? Is it our flesh? Can we love them in our own strength? Can the flesh produce any works acceptable to God? Can we practice agape love in and of ourselves? Absolutely not! Jesus says, "Without me ye can do nothing" (John 15:5). It is Jesus in us (Col. 1:27) who empowers us to live for God. Any righteousness, holiness, humility, honesty, integrity, etc., that we have always comes from Jesus' enabling. When we love all men in obedience to His commandment, who exactly is loving them through us? It is Jesus. We see that, not only is God our example in loving *all people*, He also loves them through us! It is folly to say God commanded us to love everyone, but He doesn't.

But you ask, "Didn't God say He loved Jacob but hated Esau in Romans 9:13?" Yes, He did. He was speaking of His choice of Jacob over Esau as the father of the nation of Israel. "But aren't the terms pretty strong?" Yes they are. Jesus used the same term (miseo-"to hate") when He said in Luke 14:26 that in order to serve Him we must hate our father and mother and our whole family! Do we really believe we are supposed to hate our parents in the normal sense of this term? Of course not. Neither context is speaking of a malicious hostility or a plan to hurt. It is speaking of an absolutely rigid and unchangeable choice of one person over another within a certain context. Jacob was immutably chosen as father of the nation, and Esau was soundly rejected for this role. Similarly, Luke 14 is showing us that God must absolutely be the number one Person in our lives, even if it comes to rejecting those who might try to impede this.

What of Paul, who describes his intense sorrow and great burden that lost Israel be saved in Romans 9:1-3? His desire was so great, he was actually willing to take their place in Hell! Do you honestly believe this burden was conjured up by his flesh? Are Calvinists correct that God did not share this self-sacrificial compassion? Would you dare to say anyone else but Christ in Him was the generator of this great love? Did Paul love better than his example, Jesus? Hardly! The inevitable conclusion is that God loves even those He knows won't be saved to the *fullest and deepest boundaries of agape love*; and His will and purpose were always to save them.

Let me pause here to head off any misunderstanding of what I'm referring to when I speak of Jesus loving through us. A Calvinist might say, "See there; you are agreeing that we only ever do what Jesus decided we would do. We have no free will." That is not what I'm saying at all. We've already seen and will continue to see that that definition of God's sovereignty is just not supported by the Bible. However, Galatians 5 talks of the two kinds of fruit we can produce: that of the flesh, and that of the Spirit. Love is a fruit of the Spirit. That is where He enables us to produce works acceptable to God as we choose to yield to Him. Our love to people must come out of our relationship with Him. It cannot be a fleshly work.

So it is a stark contradiction of the Bible and the nature of God to say He loves only a group He predestined to Heaven. His love for the rebellious is real and deep. It is their own refusal to believe that keeps them from being saved. John 3:16, the most well-known verse in the Bible teaches this, if you will just read it and believe it. "For God so loved the world, that He gave His only begotten Son, that whosoever believes in Him, should not perish, but have everlasting life." Does this show a God that is picking them out and saving them based on absolutely nothing that they do or believe? No! Calvinists completely shred this passage. It is unrecognizable by the time they get done with it. They insist that when a person believes, it is because God already decided they would, and has placed the faith in them apart from their will. He essentially believes for them. They are not *saved because they believe* as the passage says; they *believe because they have already been saved.* The natural cause and resulting effect clearly and simply meant here is twisted completely backwards by them. Nothing really means what it says. If we can't trust what God is saying here, how can we trust any part of the Bible? Maybe everything means the opposite of what it says! Why would God have even put this "offer" in here? What possible purpose could it serve if man cannot choose to believe?

What is the definition of the *world*? It is obvious to anyone but a Calvinist that it means *everyone in the world.* Matthew 13:38 includes the children of the wicked one as well as His own in defining the *world*. God loves them too. John 7:7 shows it includes them that hate God. Other passages include John 6:33,51; 14:17; 15:19; 17:14; Rom. 12:2; I John 3:13. There are many other such passages showing that when the word "world" is used, not only does it mean everyone, there is even an emphasis on *those who don't know God*. Christians are seen as having come out of the world to salvation. The Bible teaches that Jesus' intention was to save the world, AKA everyone in the world. (John 1:29; 3:17; 4:42; 6:33; II Corinthians 5:19)

The only out for the Calvinist is to change the definition of "world" to "the elect" *in the world*. They can't take it as the world in the normal sense, because that would mean everyone. Therefore, if God loves everyone, and He can save everyone He wants, His love would compel Him to *seek the good* of everyone and to save them all. So they are forced to find another meaning for the "world." The problem is further compounded by the fact that their definition of the world (the elect) *doesn't even include most people*, as we saw in Mathew 7:13,14. So by "the world," they can't even say, "Well, it's at least *most* of the world."

God's Word states clearly that Jesus wants to save *everyone*, and paid the price for *all*. Acts 10:34,35 teaches that He is no respecter of persons. (He is not partial regarding salvation.) I John 2:2 says He is the propitiation, *not just for the saved*, but for the **whole world**. Hebrews 2:9 says He tasted death for **every man**. II Peter 3:9 says He is not willing that any should perish, but that **all** should come to repentance. John 12:32 says Christ draws **all** men unto Him. That is speaking of the offer of salvation. John 1:7-9 teaches that Jesus came that **all men** might believe, and that He gives light (spiritual illumination) to **every man in the world**. Titus 2:11 teaches that God's grace has appeared to **all men**. Luke 19:10 says Christ came to save "that which was lost." What was lost? Was it just the elect, or was it all men? If it was all men, then Christ came to seek and save **all men**. II Corinthians 5:14,15 teaches that Jesus died for **all that were dead**. Well, *everyone* started out dead in sin.

Read I Timothy 2:4 that declares that His will is for **all men** to be saved. Look at it honestly and carefully. Try to make it mean "some." It is not possible. Read Romans 5:18, which is contrasting Adam's act that brought death on **all** men, to Jesus' act, which brought life to **all** men. It is made crystal clear that the free gift came upon the same "all" as the "all" Adam condemned. Calvinists *have to accept* that all means all when talking about those under death, but they refuse to accept the other "all" regarding those Christ died for. It's in the same sentence!

Calvinists adamantly redefine "all" as "all the elect," not all people. The normal and natural meaning is rejected because it is the only way to protect their doctrine. It begs the question, "If God wanted our Calvinist brothers and sisters to understand "all men" when He says "all men," what more could He possibly have said? Apparently, *nothing* would prevent them from changing it. "Whole world" must be "the elect only." It simply cannot be allowed to mean what it says. Could God not have said "the elect" instead of "the world" if that's what He really meant?

Calvinists are forced to define "all" as "many," "some," "all kinds of people," or "all the elect" in order to make their position tenable. They seem good at redefining. But an honest reading of these passages in their contexts makes it quite evident that God is speaking of *all people*. Besides, what would be the point of saying over and over, "God's will is to save the elect?" or "He is not willing that the elect perish." By very definition of "the elect" (all those whom God chose to be saved), it is already clear that God's will is for them to be saved! To Calvinists, He is essentially saying, "It is my will to save all those whom I have chosen to save." What a useless statement! To put it in the vernacular, "Duh!" However, if He is declaring that He wants all people to be saved, even though they won't, then we see manifested a profound truth about the love and mercy of God. He truly does love His enemies, not in just in word but in deed. The provision was made and the genuine offer was extended to *all*.

As previously mentioned, many, maybe most Calvinists don't even try to say God loves the non-elect. They are the more logical ones with regard to their own doctrine. However, some actually (and futilely) attempt to explain how He does love them, *in a way*. I would sure hate to be in this position of trying to explain how God "loves" the people He has predestined to burn alive forever because He wanted to. John MacArthur, in his book, "The God Who Loves," answers the question of the nature of God's love for those He has not elected. Notice the very careful wording designed to protect God's reputation and minimize the true horror of what He has really done to them. His words are in bold face. I have inserted my comments in regular type between his paragraphs.

The fact that some sinners are not elected to salvation is no proof that God's attitude toward them is utterly devoid of sincere love. We know from Scripture that God is compassionate, kind, generous, and good even to the most stubborn sinners. Who can deny that these mercies flow out of God's boundless love? Yet it is evident that they are showered even on unrepentant sinners.

He puts on the best possible spin. He uses "*some*" sinners, when the reality is "*most*." Notice the word "utterly." He apparently means, "See there. He is not *completely* without *any* love for them! He must have at least a smidgen of feeling for them." I would like to ask MacArthur what exactly are these great "mercies" that are being "showered." These people have been condemned to burn alive with no hope before they were born! That's mercy and boundless love? How could anyone make that statement!? Even if He felt a *little* something for them, what good or possible relevance comes from it? Why even attempt to say He feels anything?! How does that help them? It is meaningless. He is still sending them to a place of pure hate and agony! If you were kidnapped and tortured, would you tell the police the criminal was a loving person if you happened to discern he was kind of conflicted as he did unspeakable things to you?

I want to acknowledge, however, that explaining God's love toward the reprobate is not as simple as most modern evangelicals want to make it. Clearly there

is a sense in which the psalmist's expression, "I hate the assembly of evildoers" (Ps. 26:5) is a reflection of the mind of God. "Do I not hate those who hate Thee, O Lord? And do I not loathe those who rise up against Thee? I hate them with the utmost hatred; they have become my enemies" (Ps. 139:21-22). Such hatred as the psalmist expressed is a virtue, and we have every reason to conclude that it is a hatred God Himself shares. After all, He did say, "I have hated Esau" (Mal. 1:3; Rom. 9:13). The context reveals God was speaking of a whole race of wicked people. So there is a true and real sense in which Scripture teaches that God hates the wicked.

Hatred is a virtue!? Can he be serious!!? That means if I know someone hates God I'm supposed to hate *him!* I guess we're just ignoring Matthew 5:44 now! Does he go to the New Testament, the guide for Christian life in the Church Age, where neither Paul, nor any other writer even hinted that we should have anything but the deepest love for *everyone*, including our enemies? No. He goes to the Old Testament, where divine revelation is still very limited and incomplete. He quotes David, God's warrior, who enacted His bloody sentence of judgment against extremely wicked nations under God's theocracy. It is quite natural that David would have feelings of hatred toward these nations with which he was at war. He was never taught to love his enemies. *Never* is it indicated that this was an example for us. McArthur makes a *giant* leap from one statement about Esau that David is a model of

God's own feelings; then extends it to include all non-elect! He then invalidates his original argument by stating God **hates** the wicked! I'm confused. Is he trying to make the case that God hates or loves them!? By the way, *many Old Testament gentiles ended up converting to the God of Israel.*

> **So an important distinction must be made. God loves believers with a particular love. It is a family love, the ultimate love of an eternal Father for His children. It is the consummate love of a Bridegroom for His bride. It is an eternal love that guarantees their salvation from sin and its ghastly penalty. That special love is reserved for believers alone.**

The implication is that there must be *some* love for the wicked. Hence, the word *distinction*. It is just not this particular, *special* love he has for the elect. Forget the fact that Paul's love for the rebellious was all-consuming, one hundred percent, making him wish he could go to Hell in their place! But the "love" of the God *who is His example* is simply a mild little feeling we're not even completely sure about. Since He is not going to act upon it anyway and seek their good, how could it *ever* be called love?

> **However, limiting this saving, everlasting love to His chosen ones does not render God's compassion, mercy, goodness, and love for the rest of mankind insincere or meaningless. When God invites sinners to repent and receive forgiveness (Isa. 1:18; Matt. 11:28-30), His pleading is from a**

sincere heart of genuine love. "'As I live!' declares the Lord God, 'I take no pleasure in the death of the wicked, but rather that the wicked turn from his way and live. Turn back, turn back from your evil ways! Why then will you die, O house of Israel?'" (Ezek. 33:11). Clearly God does love even those who spurn His tender mercy, but it is a different quality of love, and different in degree from His love for His own.

Yes, what a merciful God! He *ensured* they would sin, blamed them, then goes through a *truly* meaningless show of "love" and "sincerity' in which He "invites" them to an eternal life He made sure they had no power to respond to and never even bought for them! So He loves them; it is just a little different in *degree*! I'll say! I'm sure this "love" will be of great comfort to them as He lowers them into burning lava and watches them scream in unimaginable agony! Exactly what *mercy ever* took place? This is absurdity on a truly monumental scale! The things he is saying are completely irrational.

Why does MacArthur even attempt this pathetic argument that God kind of loves the non-elect. He can't even decide for himself! He states that God *loves* and *hates* them in the same argument—this in a book entitled, "The God Who Loves!" I find this astounding. He writes an **entire book** about the "matchless" love of God, and this is the best he can do! John Wesley called the Calvinist God's love for the non-elect "such love as makes your blood run cold." He was scathing in his rebukes for this heresy. MacArthur here even quotes Ezekiel

33, an Arminian proof text, as if it has any meaning at all. But the Calvinist God never gave them *any option* to do what He asks. He supposedly stands there pleading with open arms for them to come to Him when He has already decided He doesn't want them to and has made sure they cannot! Why would He do that? Is it a show to appear merciful when He is nothing of the sort? What a farce! I'm so glad I could easily write a biblically rock-solid book about a God who *truly loves all* His creatures with **everything** in Him, and whose invitation is genuine!

You will find many explanations by Calvinists to defend their positions to be similarly vacillating and incoherent. They talk so glibly of God's goodness to the non-elect. If it's so wonderful, how would *they* like to be on the receiving end of it? I seriously doubt they would call it "good" anymore. Honestly, I have asked myself many times if they even feel sorry for those billions of poor people. If so, I've never seen it come across in their writings. I've personally seen almost nothing but judgment toward the so-called non-elect. It is understandable since they think God hates *His* enemies. Why should *they* care?

Note: I know a lady who was in MacArthur's church for 13 years. She had a tremendous sense that something wasn't right, and went through times of deep depression. Church was never a place of comfort for her. It was a place she dreaded, but went at the insistence of her husband. The only God she knew of was a monster. She found tremendous relief and peace upon discovering the biblical errors of Calvinism and finally knowing that God is truly good and loving in every sense, not in the severely crippled sense of Calvinism, in which human beings

love with far more substance than God Himself. I
have read of others who similarly suffered
depression and confusion in Calvinist churches. It is
understandable when they continually hear a
contradictory message. Many do not even know
there is another way to believe; that Christendom is
not represented by Calvinism.

What can Calvinists reasonably answer to I
Timothy 4:10? This passage says He is the Savior of **all
men, especially** of those that believe. Think about it. It
says He is the Savior of two groups—all men, <u>and</u> the
subgroup of those that believe. It could not be clearer that
His role of Savior extends to those who won't be saved as
well as to those who will. The only out for the Calvinist is
to completely redefine "savior." One attempt to explain this
verse which I read went something like this. It simply
means that God gives good things to all people while they
are still alive. They are given the blessings of jobs, food,
families, etc. That was it! It was one of the most ridiculous
attempts I have ever witnessed to explain away one of the
clearest verses existent in Scripture. So now "savior" is
redefined from "one who saves" to "one who gives good
things to others before committing them to torture!" That is
not a savior! What a gross and blatant twisting of Scripture.
The *biblical* definition of Christ's role as Savior is "the One
who **saves** us from God's wrath poured out in Hell." This
gift is offered to all and truly made available to all.

In I John 2:2, John says, "And he is the propitiation
for our sins: and *not for ours only*, but also for the sins of
the *whole world*." Propitiation is "hilasmos" in the Greek.
It means an atonement. John is saying Jesus not only paid
for us, His children, He paid for the entire world! Colossian
1:20 says He reconciled "all things" to Himself. Try to
make *that* mean only the elect. II Peter 2:1 even says **He
bought the false prophets!** Were they elect?! Hardly!

Calvinists are forced to mostly ignore II Peter 2 because it destroys their doctrine. They simply cannot address it or explain it in any convincing way.

Therefore, the Calvinist doctrines of *unconditional election* and *limited atonement* are pure falsehood. One Calvinist friend even admitted to me he doesn't believe in limited atonement, because the Bible is too clear that it is wrong. He does believe, however, in unconditional election. He is not the only one. There is a subgroup of Calvinists who do reject this point, which Calvin himself never espoused to my knowledge. I find it very strange that they would admit Jesus paid for everyone, but then refused to save everyone. Does that not seem inconsistent to you? The fact is, many Calvinists, maybe most, agree with theologian Loraine Boettner in his book, "The Reformed Doctrine of Predestination" page 59, that if one point of TULIP is disproved, the whole system must be abandoned.

That makes sense, because if Jesus has paid the price for everyone, how can he send most to Hell when there is no remaining price for sin? The freewill view has no problem with this. You can pay the price of a gift for someone and still have them reject the gift. God says that without faith, it is impossible to please Him; and if people choose not to believe in Jesus' payment, they are truly left with no credit, and bound to pay it on their own all over again.

5. *Jesus was heartbroken at not being able to save all men*.

In Matthew 9:36 we see Him moved with compassion, not for the elect, or His friends, but for the multitudes, most of whom would reject Him; even cry for His crucifixion. What sense does it make to tell us He felt compassion for those He Himself had decided to send to Hell when He could have easily saved them?

Compassion is made completely meaningless by this doctrine. Most people understand compassion to be a motivation to help people if there is any way to do so. To the Calvinist, it is nothing more than a mild and useless feeling. It is truly of no consequence, help, or comfort to the so-called non-elect, and certainly no indication of goodness in God. What would you think of a doctor who found a cure for a world-wide fatal epidemic, had enough for everyone, and could easily have saved all? But instead he decides to let most of them die because he wanted to, or felt he would get glory somehow. Would you say he was a good or compassionate man because he felt sorry about it? I don't think so. Now, what would you think if he *himself* had forced the epidemic to happen in the first place?!

In Matthew 23:37 and Luke 13:34, there is no question what Jesus' will and intention was. He intensely desired to protect them and save them. He concludes, "But **ye** would not." It was truly offered and make available, but *they* rejected it. The love and compassion of the Calvinist God is nothing but a show. But, that of the *true* God is absolutely solid and genuine. *Unconditional election* is on a foundation of pure sand here, as is *irresistible grace*.

6. *The Bible is full of warnings about making the right choices.*

It seems remarkable, then, that Calvinists wish to minimize that which God *strongly* emphasizes, namely, man exercising his will to make right choices. They say that ultimately, only God's choices have any effect; but that makes a complete sham of commands like that in Deuteronomy 30:19. "I call heaven and earth to record this day against you, that I have set before you life and death, blessing and cursing: therefore **choose life**, that both thou and thy seed may live…"

Let me deviate a bit and inject here that if God offered *all* of them life, then it must have been purchased for them on the cross and truly made accessible. Calvinists have no problem saying that God, in His matchless and unspeakable "mercy," offers life to the non-elect, although neither was it purchased for them, nor will they be given the ability to receive it. Can an offer like that be called genuine? What does basic reason tell you? Could I legitimately and sincerely offer you something I had not obtained for you, had no intention of *ever* doing so, and would not even make accessible to you if I had? Try that with your wife. See if she thinks you have a heart of gold.

Let's use a concrete illustration. You are trapped in a pit dying of thirst. I come and offer you water, but I have no water for you, nor do I plan to obtain it for you. But I pretend I'll get it, and I say the words, so it must be a sincere offer, right? Aren't I a swell guy? I don't think so. What if I actually *do* get the water, but I manipulate your mind to believe it is poison so you won't receive it. I "decree" that you will not recognize it as something you need. I make you "unstable" so that you will reject it. Is that a genuine, loving, and merciful offer? Only against all reason can you say yes. Now, even if I get you the water and don't manipulate your mind, you might still refuse the offer because maybe you happen to hate me. But at least now it is a *real* offer, not the outright *lie* the Calvinist offer is.

Back on point, in Joshua 24:15, Israel was commanded to choose whom they would serve. What is the relevance if God is simply pulling puppet strings and making certain ones repent? II Timothy 2:19-21 urges man to purge himself of iniquity so that he may be an honorable vessel for the Master's use. God commands His prophet in Jeremiah 26:2,3 to preach to His people so that possibly they would turn from their evil and He could ***change His mind*** about bringing judgment on them. What sense does this make if He has already determined what they will do and what He will do? Man's choices matter! The Bible teaches again and again that he must *decide* whether to receive God's gift. If God didn't want us to believe that, **why does He say it so much?**

It is clear in many passages such as Deuteronomy 7:6; 23:5; 32:6-21 that Israel was God's chosen people. This was a nation among nations that God elected to be His special possession. It is evident that His will was to save all of them. If He were a puppet master, they would all have loved Him and served Him, albeit with a robotic love. But they made their own choices, and departed from God. "When the Lord saw it, He abhorred them…" He didn't predetermine to abhor them. It says it happened *when He saw their idolatry*. Their choices had direct consequences on their fate. God was **jealous** and **angry**. Could this have been His will? Only a crazy person intentionally pulls the wires out of a car to disable it, then gets angry when it won't run!

In Jeremiah 3:1-22, Jehovah has divorced His two wives, Israel and Judah. Only a divorced person can relate to the pain of this separation; and God employs one of the most agonizing experiences of humans to illustrate to Israel how great is *His* pain as a result of their rejection of Him. It was *their choices*, not His, that led to this. He even pleads with them to return because *even then He would take them back*. But they continued in rebellion until He was eventually compelled to bring complete judgment upon them. Does this look like something He willed, decreed, and brought about? Was He planning a divorce before the marriage?!

Deuteronomy 8:2-20 teaches that God was testing Israel so that He could do them good. "Prove" in verse 2 is from the Hebrew "nacah," which means to test. Obviously, passing was contingent on them making the right choices. A test is not a test without *real choices* being made. It is also not a *real* test if the *teacher, not the student,* is really the one making the choices. Then it is simply a rigged, dishonest, fake show. Yet, that is exactly what Calvinists believe. God has rigged everything.

Can you really see all these passages and hold that God's Word says man has no true, genuine free will, with which he frequently resists the Spirit's grace and does things God didn't plan or want? Is the idea of *irresistible grace* really on solid footing? Did God really pick who would be saved, giving man no say so? Is Calvinism really more biblically founded than the freewill position? What do *you* think?

From Adam's choice in the garden to Revelation 22:17, where whosoever **wills** can take of the water of life, the importance of man's choices cannot be overlooked. To relegate the whole concept of man's decision-making responsibility to nothing more than a puppet show where God is the only One actually making the choices is a terrible biblical error.

Read Ezekiel 18:4-32 honestly. God teaches that if a wicked man turns from his evil he will live. If a righteous man turns from his righteousness and lives a wicked life, he will die. This chapter is *all about man's choices* and the consequences, not what God has predetermined, or whom He is manipulating. The Bible is full of commands to man to choose to repent (change his mind), and turn to the One who can save Him and wants a relationship with him. This **is** the Bible. Without a doctrine regarding the importance of man's response to God's grace, the Bible has no real purpose and makes very little sense. If God saves whomever He wishes by force, He never needed to first communicate with man to bring about his salvation. He could simply have zapped him up to Heaven and explained everything later!

Let me close this section with a fundamental contradiction of Calvinism. *How is it possible for* *disobedience to take place if the Creator is the **only one** making choices?* We know that disobedience is defined as choosing to do something other than what you were commanded. But Calvinists say man has no free will. He **cannot choose**. He can only **feel like** he chose! That is not choosing! If Adam had no free will then you *cannot logically say he disobeyed*. He only ever did the will of God. He was forced to do *only* what God wanted him to do. Where is the disobedience? It is a meaningless word. *Disobedience cannot take place in a universe where the creature has no free will of its own.* But Calvinists would have us believe God made Adam sin so He could get "angry," show His righteous indignation, and demonstrate "justice." Can logic possibly be more butchered? Shouldn't God be angry with Himself?

Maybe you object saying, "But disobedience is the *action* of doing something other than what you were told to do." I ask you, "What does God always look at? Is it the action or the heart? Luke 6:45, 46 and Matthew 15:18-20 are clear that actions are nothing more than the manifestation of what is in the heart. Proverbs 21:2 says God is concerned with the heart. Now think about the fact that it is impossible to act without having made a choice of some kind. When you make a peanut butter and jelly sandwich, you made a choice to do that. When coupled with the doctrine that nothing happens except what God willed and decreed, we must conclude that God *put the choice* in Adam's heart, which resulted in the action. If we are consistent with Calvinism, Adam made no choice of his own to sin! He did only what he was preprogrammed and forced to do. Again, where is the disobedience?

7. *Evangelism and testimony make a genuine difference in eternal destinies.*

Calvinists disagree with this. They believe if I witness to people, no difference is made. If I don't witness—no difference. It is already fixed. All of the efforts of God's people to evangelize the world have no effect whatsoever on the number of people who will be in Heaven. All of our intercessory prayers for the lost are basically meaningless. So, essentially, God has commanded us to spend our lives engaged in a mission to help others, when in fact, nothing we do can or will actually help them. If they were going to be saved, they will anyway. If they are not elect, there never was any hope for them. Calvinists have even told me, "God's going to save whom He's going to save, but we're still responsible to preach the Gospel. If we don't go and preach, **we** lose the blessing!

Really? So now it is not about the horrible condition of the lost and our compassion for them and desire to see them saved impelling us to sacrifice our lives and time to help them know the good news; it is really about *us* receiving a blessing! Is this what the Bible teaches? Can we really not make a difference? Is the preaching of the Gospel about *us,* and not the terrible plight of those still lost?

If this is true, your testimony before the world doesn't matter. If you live like the devil, it won't keep anyone from being saved that would not have been lost anyway. If you strive to have a good testimony so your loved ones will be drawn to God, it will have no impact. They would have been saved anyway, or vice versa. Think about the implications of this! Has God really asked us to spend our lives doing useless work and maintaining a useless testimony?

Ezekiel 3:17-21 and 33:7-9 absolutely refute this. It makes a direct and powerful connection between the watchman who is commanded to warn people about their sins and the *results* of those warnings. It teaches that what he does makes a difference! It even says the blood of the lost is *required at his hand* if he doesn't warn them. Think about this carefully! How could a person, by any form of reasoning or logic, be held responsible for the fate of another if he never was in a position to influence that fate in any possible way? Read this passage honestly, and see if we really cannot make a difference when we preach the Gospel.

As mentioned before, in Ezekiel 22:30, God makes it crystal clear that if a man had been available to engage in intercessory prayer for Israel, He would not have destroyed them. Either this is simply a stage show, or God really does expect us to understand that prayer produces actual results that would not have happened otherwise. We need to understand that our bad testimonies can send people to Hell, and our preaching of the Gospel and prayers for the lost can be the cause of someone getting saved that otherwise would not have.

Matthew 23:13-15 is poignant. Jesus Himself credited the Pharisees with the ability to influence people's eternal destinies. He told them they not only were not entering the door of Heaven, but that they were not allowing others in that *would have entered*! How could that be possible if God's design is such that He is the *only* influence and deciding factor at the door of Heaven. He states that they were making people "children of Hell." Calvinists say only *God* makes people children of Hell. According to Jesus, the Pharisees *were making a difference in the number of people in Heaven and Hell!* They were corrupt religious leaders whose testimonies and behavior were turning people away from the kingdom of God and causing them to enter a Christless eternity.

Not only were the Pharisees an obstacle to salvation, Jesus said *riches* were turning people away from it. He declared in Matthew 19:23,24 how difficult it is for rich people to be saved. It makes sense that those who trust in their wealth will tend not to see their need for God. But Calvinists say the elect are already decided, and based on nothing about the persons chosen. So is Jesus saying it was hard for God to elect rich people!? What *possible* sense could this passage make if *unconditional election* is biblical?

If you still think we cannot make a difference, consider Proverbs 23:13,14. It teaches in no unmistakable terms that parental discipline is powerfully effective in bringing about the salvation of the child. It "will deliver his soul from hell." ("Sheol" in the Hebrew. In this context it can only mean the punitive part that is known as Hell; certainly not the Paradise part.)

Can you find a logical way to explain these passages if the destination of each person is permanently predetermined by God; and nothing or no one else has anything at all to do with it?

8. *The unpardonable sin makes impossible the position that each person's destiny is fixed and unchangeable.*

Jesus taught in Matthew 12:31-32 and Luke 12:10 that if a person blasphemes the Holy Spirit, he has committed a sin that will never be forgiven. His condemnation is sealed although he is still alive. This results in another fatal contradiction for the Calvinist doctrine. If a person is predetermined to be saved regardless of what he does, and this is irreversibly set in stone, he must not be able to commit this sin. It is irrelevant. If he is predestined to Hell, and this is equally unchangeable, it would be absurd to say that if he blasphemes the Spirit he will never be forgiven. He is *already* unforgiven and condemned to Hell anyway! His sins are not even paid for. Just try to make sense of this passage if man has no free will and everything is fixed!

Some attempt to say that this sin was only possible when Jesus was on Earth—that it no longer applies. Firstly, there is nothing here or any other place in Bible that indicates this is the case. This sin is an absolute rejection of the Spirit in defiant hatred to such a degree that He never comes and draws that person again. It is different from simply resisting or ignoring.

Secondly, *if* it applied to only *one* person at *one* point in time, it would still create an unanswerable contradiction for the Calvinist. It only takes *one* created being with a *truly free will* to annihilate the doctrine.

Thirdly, if you believe it is no longer possible for someone to insult the Holy Spirit to such a degree that they permanently lose the ability to be saved, keep reading down to the section where we see Pharoah's heart hardened. There is provided a substantial list of passages teaching that there is a passing of the time of grace for many people, even before death. This can only result from the same sin Jesus speaks of in Matthew 12 and Luke 12. In other words, they are not the only places in the Bible that speak of the blasphemy of the Holy Spirit, although different words are used. These warnings are pointless if man truly cannot choose to heed them. If you are interested in eye-witness accounts of people dying and crying out desperately that it is too late for them to be saved, despite Christians begging them to pray to Jesus, look up "Dying Testimonies of the Saved and Unsaved." There are detailed accounts of people on their deathbed testifying of a time when they were under terrible conviction of the Spirit, but rejected Him so strongly that He never came again. They are left with no hope, dying in horror as they begin to feel God's wrath even before the soul leaves the body.

Without the Spirit's drawing, no one can come to Jesus. (John 6:44) Thankfully, in chapter 12, He promises to draw *all* men. "Draw" is the *same Greek word* in both places. If you have not been saved, please cherish and respond in humility to that moment, or moments, when they come to you. You never know when the last one will be. Although God initially loves everyone and deeply desires to save them, there will come a point, if salvation is rejected, when love turns to pure hate and vengeance. That is what Hell is. (II Thessalonians 1:7-9) I do not maintain that God continues to love those upon whom this sentence is already passed. There are people alive right now whose hellish eternity is certain and unchangeable. My dad met a man who can no longer be saved. This man, wishing he could change his mind and be saved, could describe exactly when he crossed the line and knew he was condemned.

We see *unconditional election* and *irresistible grace* once again proven false—and by extension, *limited atonement* as well.

9. Calvinism makes Satan completely irrelevant.

As we know, the Bible contains warnings about the devil, and the dangers of heeding him. I Peter 5:8,9 says, "Be sober, be vigilant; because your adversary the devil, as a roaring lion, walketh about, seeking whom he may devour." Calvinists say everyone at this very moment is either elect, and cannot avoid Heaven, or not elect, and cannot avoid Hell. Yet the Bible warns that we can be devoured by the devil if we are not vigilant. If Calvinism is correct, and I am elect, I'm in no danger from the devil regarding eternity; and if I am not elect, I'm going to Hell regardless of what the devil does or my response to him. What then, is the reason or relevance of the warnings about this devil, who cannot influence the eternal destiny of even one person? There was *never anything* he could have done to me!

In II Corinthians 4:4, the devil deceives unbelievers so they will continue in unbelief. According to the Bible, Satan *is* relevant. He draws people into unbelief that might have believed without his predations. Clearly, if the Pharisees could actually influence the number of people in Hell, then Satan can too. In other words, he is completely relevant; and *unconditional election* and *irresistible grace* are again proven false.

Calvinists insist God uses means, and that's how we explain this. He's using the devil to make His will happen. But that makes no sense. If I'm non-elect, God never needed the devil to make me reject Him. I could not *possibly* have received Him anyway! The same can be said in every scenario in which they talk about God using "means."

10. Calvinism makes it impossible to make sense of the Biblical teaching that we were children of wrath and on our way to Hell before being saved.

The Bible is clear that there was a time in the Christian's life when he or she was on the way to Hell. Ephesians 2:2-6 describes us as all having been children of wrath (on our way to Hell) before being saved. We were separated from God (on our way to Hell). I Corinthians 6:9-11 states that the unrighteous shall not inherit the kingdom of God, further concluding that every Christian was one of these people at one time (on our way to Hell). Colossians 3:6-7 as well as numerous other passages reveals that before we were saved, our destiny was Hell. If we had died, that's where we would have gone.

But a doctrine that states our destinies were immutably predetermined would make this conclusion impossible. Calvinists believe that the Christian's destination was decided and sealed long before he was ever born. He had no part in the decision. There was never a possibility that he was going to Hell. He could **never** have gone to Hell if he tried. So if there was never a time in his life when he could have died and gone to Hell, then he was *never a child of wrath*! There was never a time when he was counted as an enemy of God and destined to judgment and eternal condemnation. So if the Calvinist wants to be consistent with his own doctrine, he cannot say, "Thank God, I was on my way to Hell, I was a child of wrath, but then God saved me and gave me a new hope and a new destination."

11. *If Calvinism is biblically sound, there will be no regrets for people in Hell.*

To make this point clear, I am referring to regret over one's poor choices or wrong actions that caused unnecessary suffering. For instance, a person gives into road rage and ends up killing someone. He sits in prison regretting his terrible choice and wishing he could go back in time and make a different one. Prison inmates typically have this regret. Now think about the implications of Calvinism carefully. It teaches Adam was essentially forced to sin by God's design. It was decided and decreed. So, Adam, *had to fall.* He was <u>prevented from obeying.</u> He was our representative. We were in him, and fell with him and death passed upon all men (Romans 5:12). Consequently, we never had a choice but to be sinful, just as Adam didn't.

So now the theological chain of Calvinism leads us to the lost person predestinated to Hell. According to Calvinist teaching, he never had an option not to sin, not even in Adam. He is lost, without hope, and there is absolutely nothing he could ever have done at any time to avoid it. He never had any alternative but to come into existence for the singular purpose of being tortured, burning alive in Hell for all the billions and billions of years of eternity. One hundred billion years later, he is still screaming and burning, and will never find an end to his suffering. One hundred trillion years later, he has not suffered even one minute of eternity.

If this hideous doctrine were true, he would have at least one consolation. Although he will be in agony, and desperately wishing to get out, he will have no regrets!

How could he? There was *nothing* he could *ever* have done *differently* at *any time* to avoid this fate. He was never allowed the power nor the possibility of choosing righteousness. He was railroaded into Hell because the Creator wanted him there. He would know that what happened to him was simply destined to be. He is a victim of an omnipotent Being who had planned to burn him from the beginning. It is just something that happened. Can you honestly believe that the loving and merciful God of the Bible is telling us that *this* was His plan? Is this how He demonstrates justice!? I submit it is impossible. It simply does not line up with the scriptural depiction of God's love, mercy, and justice.

The fact is, we, as beings created in God's image, were given a conscience and an understanding of the concept of justice, by God Himself. This causes us to innately recognize that any judicial system is predicated upon *choices*. There is no justice without options. We don't throw people in jail for doing something they had no other choice but to do. No jury except a corrupt one knowingly convicts a person when it is established that there was absolutely no other outcome he or she could have brought about. Consequently, prison and regret go hand-in-hand, because the convicted know they didn't have to be there. *Regret is a result of justice being administered for poor choices.* The God who is the source of all justice teaches us that those who go to Hell didn't have to, but chose to have pleasure in unrighteousness (II Thess. 2:12). "Why will ye die?" the prophet asks in Ezekiel 33. The condemned will know they are in that place justly, in every sense of the word. For all eternity they will suffer in endless regret, knowing that the Lamb of God died for them and extended His incredible mercy and grace. They could have been in Heaven, but they rejected His priceless gift, for which they must face His wrath without end. Think about it honestly. Is Hell *true justice* if the damned had no alternative and therefore regret cannot exist there? I claim the Calvinist *justice* is completely fake—another word's meaning twisted, manhandled, and destroyed.

Should you object by saying he will be led or allowed to think he could have made the right choice, so his condemnation is just; well, now you're talking about regret under false pretenses and deception. I can't believe a Calvinist would entertain that thought. I think we all agree God is not dishonest.

Let me infuse an additional thought a little off topic. Some Calvinists, although not all, say God did not predestine the non-elect to Hell. He simply *passed over them* when selecting who would go to Heaven. This seems to be a tactic to protect the "loving" reputation of God.

Let's examine this. So, presumably, God didn't actually pick people to go to Hell; He just sort of wasn't paying much attention to their blurry faces in His peripheral vision as He searched the crowd for His favorites. He didn't have that much to do with them going to Hell. They just kind of went there by default.

Let's return to rationality and logic, and think about a particular person going to Hell. Our God knows everything intimately about this person. He formed him in the womb. He knows all his thoughts, hopes, and dreams. He could not know more if this were the only person in the world, and He focused only on him. Now it's decision time. Will He pick him to go to Heaven? If He doesn't, does that mean He just sort of ignored Him and let Him drift off into Hell? Let's be sensible. If He deliberately chose not to let him into Heaven, explain how that is not a predestination to Hell. Does God "send" people to Hell; or do they just sort of land there because there is no other place to go? II Thessalonians 1:8 says they are objects of His vengeance. Matthew 13:41 shows His angels actually target the wicked and cast them into Hell. God sends them! Calvinists themselves say nothing happens but what God *specifically* predetermines. So if God predestines people to Heaven, He *absolutely* predestines people to Hell!

Maybe you object, saying the Bible doesn't use that exact word regarding Hell. How does that make any difference at all? Do we believe in the Trinity? Yes. Does that mean the word "trinity" is in the Bible? No. There are many words that don't appear in the Bible but still represent biblical facts.

If you are of Calvinist belief, then, please at least have the consistency and rationality to admit you are compelled to believe God deliberately and purposefully predestined people to Hell just as deliberately as He did to Heaven. It was no accident or afterthought. Say it as it is. I respect the fact that John Piper openly adheres to this doctrine of double predestination, although I certainly don't agree with it.

12. *Calvinism makes the Judgment Seat of Christ meaningless.*

The Bible tells us there will be a judgment of believers, in which they are rewarded for their good works, and experience loss for the bad. (Romans 14:10; I Corinthians 3:11-15; II Corinthians 5:9,10; Galatians 6:7; Ephesians 6:8; Revelation 22:12) I asked a Calvinist friend what significance a reward system has when God, never the Christian, decided what they were going to do for Him, or how dedicated they would be. He was a studied man who was actually counseling me at the time. He seemed blind-sided, and had no answer when I showed him the Judgment Seat in I Corinthians 3. He had once told me in passing that God had not placed in his wife's heart to be a dedicated Christian like He had in him; and he just needed to accept that. It was the old idea that we never do anything that God Himself didn't decide *we* would decide. So naturally this was a conundrum for him.

Calvinists can't seem to stand the idea that we could ever actually make a right choice, from salvation to good works. If I make a choice to do something out of love for God that He didn't decree for me, then I might get some credit and be counted deserving of some glory. How dare anyone but God get any glory! Yet that is what is happening when God rewards His children in front of the whole assembly. Romans 8:17 says the plan is for us to be glorified together with Christ.

I ask you, what possible meaning could a Heavenly tribunal have when God was the only one deciding *who* would do *what* the entire time? The whole thing would be a joke, nothing but a ridiculous show. God would be rewarding whatever good He decided each puppet would do, and punishing whatever bad He decided they would do. Rewards are understood by non-Calvinists to be a motivation to serve God with all our hearts. What place could they possibly have when every person's dedication level and service was preprogrammed by God? Logic gives most people a natural understanding that rewards only make sense when true free will exists, in which God's children do things that He *didn't specifically program them to do.*

Read II Chronicles 1:7-12, in which God granted Solomon anything he wanted to name, and Solomon asked for wisdom instead of what most people would have asked for. God said, "Because this was in thine heart, and thou hast not asked riches, wealth, or honour, nor the life of thine enemies, neither yet hast asked long life; but hast asked wisdom and knowledge for thyself, that thou mayest judge my people, over whom I have made thee king: Wisdom and knowledge is granted unto thee; and I will give thee riches, and wealth, and honour, such as none of the kings have had that have been before thee, neither shall there any after thee have the like."

According to Calvinism, Solomon only played out God's *decree* that he would ask for this. I wonder then, why God is so pleased and proud of his child, as if he, Solomon, had made this decision on his own. The natural reading and understanding is that this was God rewarding His child because of a choice *he,* Solomon, made! It should be quite clear this didn't happen because of a decree, or a circuit board God had implanted in Solomon. *He* made this decision, not God! Just as I see the Calvinist justice system to be fake and contrived, I see the reward system to be equally fake. As with the people in Hell, there will be no regrets on the part of God's people, because each will know that he or she only did what they were preprogrammed to do, and could not possibly have done otherwise. The song that says, "I'll wish I had given Him more" becomes another farce. The whole thing reminds me of a boy playing with toy soldiers. I find no more depth than that in the Calvinist system.

This finishes my claims.

Now let's look at some typical objections and favorite passages of Calvinists. Is there a way to reasonably answer them? I believe there is.

What of the passages that teach God chose us, predestinated us, hardens the hearts of some, etc?

Anyone who honestly studies all aspects of man's will in the Bible, and how it ties in with the sovereignty of God, will see that, although we can arrive at certain definite conclusions on smaller points, no one can completely piece together the big picture. I certainly don't claim to have the answers to every question. For instance, I don't know why more light is given to some than others. The reason I am not a Calvinist is because, after extensive study on the concept of election as presented in the Bible, I have concluded, as have many others, that the Calvinist view of it produces major inconsistencies that cannot be reconciled, and ultimately precludes the possibility of making sense of the Bible as a whole if carried to its logical conclusions.

I will, however, examine briefly some biblical principles that I believe can shed some light on confusing passages. Before continuing, keep in mind that interpretation of the Bible must *always* be done with the *whole* Bible in mind. The Bible interprets the Bible. This is Bible Exegesis 101. All hermeneutics (bible study methods) classes will repeat that. For some reason, God did not choose to give us a thorough exposition of each doctrine in any one place in His Word. It is almost always necessary to see many passages in order to formulate a complete and correct doctrinal position. Many of these passages seem contradictory at first glance.

Let's look at an example. Colossians 1:15 says Jesus is the firstborn of every creature. Now, if you were looking at this verse, and it was the only verse in the Bible you had ever seen, what would be your conclusion about the eternal existence of Christ? A natural reading would seem conclusive that Jesus was born into existence (created) at some point. This is not speaking of the virgin birth because it did not happen before every other creature was born. The Jehovah's Witnesses love this verse because it seems to back up their position that Jesus is a created being, not God. When we tell them this is not what it means, their opinion is that we are evading a clear teaching of Scripture.

However, Christians know that the evidence throughout the Bible that Jesus is God, equal with the

Father, is so overwhelming, that they are forced to seek another explanation that not only accommodates this passage, but all others that address the identity of Christ as well. In other words, interpretation of this passage must not violate the clear teachings of other passages. Therefore, our interpretation of Colossians 1:15 must be limited to an understanding that it is not speaking of how Christ came into existence, but is simply elevating Him to the high and privileged position of the firstborn son as all Jews of the time would have understood. The firstborn son was the heir who would receive double what other sons would. He was also the head of the home upon the father's death, as well as the spiritual leader. Colossians is telling us that Christ is our big Brother, the elevated One, the preeminent One.

Another favorite of the same cult is John 14:28, in which Jesus says, "My Father is greater than I," seemingly teaching that He is inferior to the Father and must be a created being. But the Bible overwhelmingly contradicts this, so we are forced to conclude that He is only speaking of His time on this earth, during which He laid aside His divine attributes, as Philippians 2:5-8 indicates.

Ecclesiastes 9:10 could be taken as conclusive that when you're dead, you're dead; there is no life after death, at least not immediately. However, Christians know that Paul teaches that to be absent from the body is to be present with the Lord (II Corinthians 5:8). This is supported too strongly to dismiss as obscure. So we dig deeper and understand that Ecclesiastes is based on the perspective of those "under the sun," i.e., those still alive, who just see a dead body that can no longer work. It is not speaking from the perspective of those in the afterlife.

Every major doctrine must be formulated this way. There are almost always verses that seem to contradict, but in faith we accept that God's Word is not inconsistent; and we strive to seek the explanation that remains after taking all passages into account and eliminating those interpretations that are clearly impossible. We instinctively understand the concept of "weight" as well. When two verses seem to contradict twenty, the two verses should accommodate the twenty. When one doctrine has far more support than another contradictory one, the one with more weight should be favored. I see the freewill position as a mountain compared to the mole hill of Calvinism. Still, there is that pesky mole hill.

Before we look at some of the favorite passages of Calvinists, let's review these conclusions which we have seen are based on very strong and clear Scriptural support, and which must be accommodated in interpreting other passages.

1. Adam was not somehow engineered defective so that he had to sin. He alone made this choice. He could have chosen to obey.

2. Although God is sovereign, He has chosen to allow latitude for man's choices to interfere with His will. Obviously, this has limits, and God's plan and design will ultimately accomplish all His purposes.

3. God's plan was to save everyone, and He died for all men. He did not unconditionally condemn most people to Hell and save the rest by force.

4. Man has a truly free will. He can and does frequently resist the grace of God.

5. Man's choices are of great importance in the Bible. God does not deal with man as with a puppet, manipulating his will. He has chosen to reason with him, using love and the fear of coming judgment to motivate him to submit.

6. Evangelism, prayer, and our testimonies make a definite difference in the salvation of souls. We can serve God knowing our labor is not in vain. Our attention should be

directed in compassion toward the plight of lost souls, not mainly on ourselves and the blessings *we* will receive for preaching the Gospel.

7. The Calvinist doctrines of: *unconditional election, irresistible grace*, and *limited atonement* create manifold contradictions when analyzed holistically in the Bible.

Romans 9:15-23 is the pillar of the Calvinist doctrine. Although there are other passages that can seem to lend credence to their position, this is the strongest one. It speaks of God hardening Pharaoh's heart, causing some to conclude that he was never given a chance to repent, but was simply created for the purpose of being used as an example before being condemned. Honestly, if this were the only passage of the Bible I had ever seen, I would probably believe what Calvinists teach. We've already seen that this position, although seemingly apparent from the wording in Romans, would contradict the clear and numerous statements to the contrary that God makes throughout the Bible. So, just as we did with Colossians 1:15, we are forced to dig deeper and find an interpretation that is consistent with the *whole* Bible.

Before talking about Pharaoh, though, I want to point out that the context of this passage is *not* individual election to salvation. Context is always king, and you cannot ignore it or you will go wrong. The context is Gentiles and Israel. God chose Jacob's descendants as His chosen people, and rejected other nations for this privilege, including the descendants of Esau. It is not talking about how salvation works. He said Esau would serve Jacob, which never happened individually. However, Esau's nation, Edom, did eventually serve Israel. In fact, God brought severe judgment on them for attacking Israel. He pronounces judgment against them in Amos and Obadiah and states they will be wiped out. We are nowhere given permission to assume not a single Edomite ever believed in Yahweh.

Why does God harden the hearts of some people?

The Bible does teach this. Does it mean He deliberately makes them evil and unrepentant so that they are never given a chance to be saved? The Bible contradicts this. So what does it mean that God hardened Pharaoh's heart?

In Exodus 5:2 we see that Pharaoh rejected Jehovah *before* the later statement that God hardened his heart. The Hebrew word in Exodus which is translated "hardened" means to "strengthen." There is a principle given in God's Word in which He actually turns against a rebellious person who rejects His grace and mercy. There is a cut-off point from which there is no return, and after which the person becomes a vessel of wrath. After that, God will sometimes strengthen the individual's resolve to rebel, allowing him to be even more rebellious. Although his moment of grace has passed, and he can no longer be saved, he can be a tool for God's use. God literally strengthened Pharaoh's ability to stand up to Him and continue saying, "No!" in the face of the horrible plagues God was dishing out for the destruction of Egypt. God did not originate this rebellion, but He did strengthen what already existed. Pharaoh would have caved much sooner but for this supernatural strength. God wanted him to go the distance so He that could continue to manifest His great power to the world by the plagues. In light of the massive evidence in the Bible that God has provided salvation for all, and desires the salvation of all, I must reject the idea that Pharaoh *never* at any time had an opportunity to repent. There *must* have been a moment when he fully and finally rejected the offer of God's grace before God's love for him turned to hatred and rejection, and at which time God purposed to make an example of him.

There were times when the moment of grace passed for Israel, and God actually blinded them (Isaiah 6:9-12). They were the chosen people, but the moment came when God withdrew the opportunity to be saved. Jesus did the same thing in Matthew 13:11-15 after He had been so ferociously rejected in Matthew 12:24-32. From that point He began to deliberately hide the truth from the rebellious, and reserve it for those who genuinely wanted it.

For further study on the passing of the time of grace, see Genesis 6:3; Isaiah 63:17; Micah 3:4; Jeremiah 7:13-16; Proverbs 1:23-31; I Samuel 28:6; Matthew 12:30-32; Romans 1:24-28; and II Thessalonians 2:7-12. It is very dangerous to play around with the Holy Spirit. There are people who have crossed the line and can no longer be saved although they are still alive. These are truly dead men and women walking.

Isaiah 55:6 says, "Seek the Lord while He may be found." This shows there is a time when He *can* be found, and a time when He *cannot*. This destroys *unconditional election* and *irresistible grace*. The non-elect *never could have* found him, and the elect *could not help* but find Him. What a useless and senseless warning if Calvinism is true!

What about the Potter making vessels both for honor and dishonor in Romans 9?

If you accept the Calvinist interpretation of Romans 9, you will have contradicted much of the Bible. You must then *force* a lot of passages to line up by twisting and manipulating them as we have seen. Some traditionalists, however, are made uneasy by this chapter. After all, when exposited by a Calvinist, it can seem to say what they want you to believe. But, what if there is a plausible non-Calvinist interpretation that lines up with God's Word and

His nature in general. If we entirely wipe the determinist view from our minds, look at the context, and start fresh, we will see that another view is not only possible, but entirely plausible. Keep in mind that interpretations of this text come in different flavors among both Calvinists and non-Calvinists. My aim is not to convince you of every detail in the particular view I'm going to put forth. Rather, it is simply to show you that this chapter cannot be touted as fatal to the freewill view; that there are viable alternatives.

I recommend that you take time to read the entire book of Romans. You will notice that Paul makes clear time after time after time that salvation is **conditional** on *faith*, not works. Israel has stumbled because of unbelief. But Calvinists force chapter 9 to teach that salvation is **unconditional** and based only on God's choosing who will be saved. Their view blatantly contradicts both the content before chapter nine and after.

First, as we've seen, Calvinists generally don't believe God shares Paul's love and compassion for the lost in verses 1-3. But he is writing under God's inspiration! How does that make sense? Now let's see what Paul wants to show as he continues. Calvinists say he is showing us here how salvation works; that God alone chooses which individuals will be saved based on absolutely nothing they do. But this chapter is not about that. In chapter 3, Paul raises the question whether God is just for taking vengeance on His chosen people, and if this means He will not fulfill His promises to Abraham regarding his descendants. He continues dealing with this in chapter nine. Here he makes the case that God's word to Abraham that the world would be blessed by his descendants has not been invalidated because of Israel's disobedience (verse 6). They were the carriers of the Word of God, and the lineage from whom the Messiah would come, as verses 4 and 5 sum up. That has not changed, and neither has God's promises for future Israel. He is not done with them, though it may appear so.

Paul demonstrates how only the seed of Abraham who came from Israel (Jacob) are the elect for this task. The branches starting with Ishmael and Esau are excluded (verses 7-13). Please note the word "elect" simply means chosen for some purpose. It has nothing to do with salvation in and of itself. It is used in many ways and contexts in the Bible. Calvinists have a tendency to latch onto it as automatically meaning chosen for salvation, although here it is too clear even for them that this is not the case. This is not referring to the only group in the world chosen for salvation, as they would have to agree. Paul also takes the opportunity to show how this physical distinction between nations is an illustration, or analogy, showing the distinction between those who are God's children and those who are not. Just because one is an Israelite does not mean he or she is automatically saved. There are Abraham's physical seed, but there are also Abraham's spiritual seed. The spiritual seed are the actual children of the promised redemption. This is also seen in Romans four. As Abraham believed God and it was counted for righteousness, he is the spiritual father of all who believe. (See also Galatians chapter 3 and 4, especially 3:29)

The question arises in verse 14, "Is God unrighteous to leave the other nations out of this blessing of being God's chosen people?" Is it fair that He doesn't treat them all the same? He rejected Esau's descendants from being in this group. In verse 15, Paul's answer is that God is free to make His own choices in showing mercy. Keep in mind that mercy does not necessarily equal salvation. Although He eventually wiped out Edom, He did not do so to Israel in Exodus 32, 33 when they deserved the same. Paul quotes Exodus 33:19, which is God's declaration right after the terrible sin of the golden calf. God says, "[I] will show mercy on whom I will show mercy." In response to Moses' pleading, God refrains from the destruction He thought to wreak. He is saying that He alone has the right to make these decisions. He decides what to do with each nation and how He will work His plan. The "it" in verse 16 is not salvation; it is His plan given in verse 11. This is not talking in any way about election to salvation.

Remember, He is originally talking about the reprobates in Israel. How could His chosen people have been this rebellious and blind? We have seen that God often hardens people after they have persisted in rebellion. The same thing that happened to Pharaoh has happened to the Jews many times, including in the days of Jesus when they crucified Him (Romans 11:1-10; Deuteronomy 29:4; Isaiah 6:9, 29:10; Jeremiah 5:21). This is Paul's point in verses 17 and 18. What happened to Pharaoh has happened to Israel. This goes back to his point that one is not safe from destruction simply because he is a Jew.

Now, in verse 19, there is an objector who says, "How can God find fault with those He has hardened?" Calvinists quickly equate this to a traditionalist questioning the Calvinist view of election to salvation. That doesn't even remotely fit the context of this whole passage, or all of Romans for that matter. The context points to someone objecting to God blaming people He has given over to their evil and blinded. He used Pharaoh's evil works to show His glory. He used the hardened Pharisees and leadership of the Jews to crucify His Son to save the world. He is using part of Israel, the vessels of wrath who have fitted themselves to destruction, or the bad clay, to accomplish His plan and bless the rest of Israel and also the Gentile church, the vessels of mercy, or the good clay. God is free to choose the time He hardens someone or doesn't. He is righteous in using the rebellious to accomplish His purposes. Paul replies that we have no right as the clay and miniscule beings to question the Potter. He will do as He wills.

Calvinists insist the clay is incapable of doing anything. It is dead and passive. But that is absolutely false. Remember, no analogy can be equated to the thing illustrated in every way. If it could, it *would be* the thing. In Jeremiah 18:1-10, which Paul is quoting here, it shows definitively that if the clay repents, God will change His mind regarding what He will do with it! In other words, they can become vessels of mercy! The Calvinist must now insist that Paul is heading in a new direction, and we can't take seriously this quote in the way it is manifested in the Old Testament. I would ask, "Then why did Paul quote from it in the first place?" Furthermore, II Timothy 2:20, 21 also specifies that the vessels *decide* whether to be vessels of honor or dishonor! They do it by deciding to be clean. God saves whom He will, but He has made clear who that is. He gives grace to the humble. (James 4:6; I Peter 5:5,6; Psalm 18:27)

Verse 22 is very strange in light of Calvinism. God is patiently putting up with the vessels of wrath. Since He supposedly *made them rebellious* with His own decrees, that means He is being longsuffering with His own will! This doctrine constantly puts God in conflict with Himself. The freewill view simply understands that He doesn't wipe out the wicked immediately, but uses them for His own purposes. Isn't that what He has been doing with the devil for thousands of years?

Calvinists love to quote the fact that the choices regarding Jacob and Esau happened unconditionally before they were born, showing that God predestines people to Heaven and Hell without regard to anything in them or about them. But that destroys justification by faith and is unfaithful to the context besides. The point is, God made the choice about who would be the father of the nation to bless the world without regard to whether Jacob or Esau deserved it or not. We are never told God started out to hate Esau. In fact in Deuteronomy 23:7, He specifically told

Israel not to detest their brother Edom. Does this sound like hatred as the Calvinists wish us to understand it? Edom later brought judgment on themselves for their choices to attack and abuse Israel.

This interpretation of Romans 9 is a pretty standard freewill view. As mentioned, there are different flavors, but the traditional view simply knows nothing about this being about individual election to salvation based on nothing anyone does, but recognizes it as Paul's explanation of what has happened to Israel and where they are in God's plan. Chapters 10 and 11 go on to show what the future holds for them, and to emphasize that God has not cast them away forever. This chapter does not at all destroy the traditional view.

One final note regarding verse 19: This is the great escape hatch for the Calvinist. When challenged with the statement that there is clearly no true justice in "making" someone evil and a vessel of wrath by predetermination, all the Calvinist has to do is say, "It says right here that you have no right to question God. If He decides someone will be evil and damned with no hope, we have to accept that He is still good and just even though we don't understand." At this point, any possible logic has been effectively abandoned, and a seemingly unanswerable excuse for doing so has been produced. The traditionalist now has to wonder if he or she is in danger of blaspheming if they continue to challenge the determinist view. I still remember being in shock and horror when confronted with this verse and not seeing a way out at that time. That's what precipitated my journey into this entire study, initially thinking I might have to embrace Calvinism but eventually seeing the contradictions and errors. It also produced in me a desire to help others in the same struggle.

How can we say God loves everyone when Psalms sometimes says He hates the wicked?

This is more of an answer to Calvinists who say God hates the non-elect. We've already seen that some, like MacArthur, desperately try to say He loves them, although the "love" described is nothing but sheer horror. He "offers" them a salvation He made sure they could never receive, and which He never even provided for them, so He could proceed with His plan to burn them alive.

Psalm 5:4-6 says, "For thou art not a God that hath pleasure in wickedness: neither shall evil dwell with thee. The foolish shall not stand in thy sight: thou hatest all workers of iniquity. Thou shalt destroy them that speak leasing [lies]: the Lord will abhor the bloody and deceitful man." Psalm 11:5 says, "The Lord trieth the righteous: but the wicked and him that loveth violence his soul hateth."

How can we say God loves everyone? Well, for one thing, we're all wicked so we certainly can't conclude this hatred is an exclusion of a chance to be saved. God saves wicked people! He hates what they do, and by extension, He hates what they are; but He *chose* to love His *enemies* with a sacrificial, unconditional, agape love and offer them salvation. There is no contradiction here. Romans 5:10 states clearly that we were *all* enemies of God before being saved. Thank God He overrode His hatred and showed love to the world!

He *defers* His hatred and its consequences for a time, choosing to genuinely seek our good. But, for those that refuse His love, there will come a time when He acts on this hatred and sends them to Hell, the place where His wrath is poured out without mixture. We have already seen solid biblical evidence that His love to the wicked is real, and His offer is real. It is not the fake offer of Calvinism, nor the fake love that doesn't seek the good of its object.

How can God be sovereign if man has a free will?

A favorite text of Calvinists is Isaiah 46:10, in which God says, "My counsel shall stand, and I will do all my pleasure." Calvinists have decided, for some reason, that this statement defines God's sovereignty to mean not one tiny, little thing *ever* happens that is not His will. He decreed everything. This is their most foundational belief. Every time you sin, God ordained and planned for that sin to happen, because it was His will. You were predestined to commit it. Every time you are selfish, hateful, slanderous, lustful, foul-mouthed, dishonest, etc., it is because God decreed you would do it. Every time a little child is brutally assaulted or raped, this was His will, and He made it happen. I am sorry for the terrible example, but these things need to be said. When David sinned with Bathsheba, it was God's choice. Forget the fact that God was *displeased* and blamed David. And they maintain that only what *pleases* Him happens!

Ask deeply indoctrinated Calvinists about this. Investigate for yourself and you will see I am not making this up. Along with the founders of "The Baptist Confession of Faith of 1689," they will say with a straight face, "God decides, ordains, and decrees every sin; yet He is not the author of sin. It is man's fault alone!" The contradictions of Calvinism are staggering. You might as well believe that someone who places a bomb in a public place didn't kill anyone; the bomb did!

I see this as nothing other than blasphemy. Can you imagine the pure and holy God of Isaiah 6, before the foundation of the world, making a list of all the evil, rotten, disgusting, putrid, filthy things He is going to have his creatures do? He sits there planning and assigning thousands of hand-picked sins to each human being, choosing who is going to be a rapist, a murderer, an adulterer; which pastor is going to molest a child or run off with his secretary; what individuals are going to be slaves to drugs; who is going to produce pornography; what filthy words and foul jokes he wants you to say! He commands you in I Peter 1:16 to be holy as He is holy, while ordaining exactly how you are going to violate that command. Why even give the command He is going to prevent you from obeying? What rot from hell this is! John Wesley said Calvinism makes God worse than the devil! I have to agree. What a tragedy that a doctrine would come into being among God's own children that demeans Him so and places the Holy Savior in the gutter with Satan!

Frankly, when one abandons all logic and rational thought to this degree, when words no longer mean what they mean, and new meanings are plucked out of the air, the time for debate is over. There is nothing more to say. When a person is this far gone into the twilight zone of Calvinistic irrationality, I have little hope that anything they read here or elsewhere will even begin to change their minds, although it does occasionally happen. Quite often, there is a preacher with a strong personality behind it all, indoctrinating the people, who was indoctrinated himself. To me, honestly, it seems to have cultish overtones. Disciples are prepared with carefully worded answers to every point raised against it. Those who move away from it are often ostracized and rejected by former friends; and the militant activity to convert everyone to it never ceases. I am not saying all Calvinists are this way, but the patterns I have seen strike me that way. I had a friend that I finally stopped spending time with, because he couldn't let it go. He sought every chance to raise the issue and convert me.

Back to the point, can Isaiah 46:10 *only* be taken the Calvinist way? A similar verse is Psalm 135:6. They are very general. Frankly, I look at them aghast, and find myself wondering how in the world they got all that. It is just not there short of injecting a predetermined belief system. We've already seen that such a definition of sovereignty is not even remotely supported by the Bible as a whole. How does the statement that God does whatever

He pleases lead to this? Of course He does what He pleases! No one is questioning that. How do you get from that to the conclusion that He chose and originated all of your sins?! The Bible tells us, over and over, that God was *displeased* about *many* things people did!

Could not God, in His sovereignty, decide to create a system in which His creatures have free will and are able to do something that is not *His* will? If He *decided* to do so; if that was *His pleasure*, there is nothing about that which contradicts Isaiah in any way, shape, or form. However, Calvinists have decided on *one interpretation only*. Sovereignty MUST be defined as God preordaining every single thing that happens, no matter the scope or nature. When you swat a fly, that event was decreed before the foundation of the world. Any other definition is unthinkable and unbearable.

Dr. James White, a noted Calvinist debater, even claims the reason God knows the future is *precisely* because He is the one willing and bringing everything about, including every sin. You can find him in multiple YouTube videos. Arthur W. Pink, a well-known, deceased Calvinist theologian and author, made the statement, "If God did not foreordain all things, then he could not know the future. God foreknows and knows all things because He decreed all things to be."

This is shocking to me. For one thing, the Bible *never* says that anywhere. It is an invention. Secondly, how dare a finite man think he has figured out the tiniest thing about the inner workings of God's omnipotent power? Has he also figured out how God can be simultaneously everywhere in the universe? Has he figured out how God keeps track of every atom? Is he able to explain how God can choose not to be affected by gravity, or how He created it in the first place? Does he know how God managed to create quadrillions of suns and fill the universe with them? But White and Pink declare they have unraveled the mystery of God's omniscience, and then proceed to support a doctrine on that ridiculous foundation. They have somehow ascertained God couldn't know the future *any other way*! The fact that God inhabits eternity, Isaiah 57:15, doesn't seem to mean anything.

But, God transcends time. "Is anything too hard for the Lord?" Not according to Genesis 18:14. Apparently, in the same way He is everywhere at once, He is *every time* at once. He can see the future because He is already there. He is not the weak god locked in time that James and Pink think He is. Furthermore, it not only is not our responsibility as miniscule, finite beings to figure out how God's infinite power works; it is utterly impossible.

Let's consider a world where God's sovereignty is defined as His maintaining control of His purpose regardless of what man does, but where He actually allows His plans, within preset parameters, to be altered by His creatures. This is anathema to the Calvinist. To anyone else, it is how a relationship works, which, by the way, *appears to be what God wants with us*!

Let's first view it from an intuitive perspective before looking at some Bible examples that clearly bear it out. We are beings created in God's image. As such we have an idea how He thinks, apart from our sin nature of course. We understand emotion, desire, and relationship because we got that from God. Do you really think He would find a relationship with you interesting if He were the one making you do everything you do? Every time you tell Him you love Him, He decided you would do that. Every time you thank Him, it is because He made it happen. Every time you feel something for Him, He Himself originated that, not you. If you attend Bible study, He is the one that made you go. If you bring Him a gift, you had nothing to do with it. He decreed that He would receive a gift from you. He has decided everything you will ever think and every move you will ever make, in this scenario. You never do anything for Him that originated in your own heart, from your own true free will apart from His. He is pulling the puppet strings every time you lift your hands and praise Him.

How would you like a daughter that you manipulate like that? She only ever does, says, thinks, or feels what you program in advance. You know the very next thing she will do, from scratching her elbow, to studying hard for a test, to disobeying an order, because you are the one who determined it. You will never have the joy of receiving a spontaneous expression of love from her that you didn't actually decree, plan, and make happen. Do you really think God wanted robots like this? Calvinists always insist we are not robots while asserting God alone decides *everything* we will do, say, or feel. How is this not a contradiction? What does your own intuition tell you? Does it seem even a little unrealistic to you that this puppet show is the kind of relationship our Father wanted with His creatures? He gave us earthly fathers to show us how His relationship with *us* works. **But the Calvinist view of divine fatherhood has *no similarity whatsoever* to earthly fatherhood.**

What does the Bible say? The passages in the second claim of this treatise alone are conclusive that man can certainly go outside God's will and alter His plans. But let's look more closely. There are solid indications that God adapts what He does to what His creatures do; that He, in fact, often has a plan B. Let's revisit Numbers for a closer look at Israel's refusal to enter the promise land.

Please read chapters 13 and 14. It says Israel sent twelve spies to look at the land and report back. All of them except Joshua and Caleb persuaded the people that they could not possibly defeat the giants they had seen there. Instead of believing in God's power to give them victory, they rebelled and refused God's great gift of a wonderful dwelling place, even accusing Him of bringing them there to die. To say God was angry is a gross understatement. He was going to kill them all and start over.

He said to Moses, "How long will this people provoke me? and how long will it be ere they believe me, for all the signs which I have shewed among them? I will smite them with the pestilence, and disinherit them, and will make of thee a greater nation and mightier than they." Only through Moses' pleading did God spare them. Could you honestly declare that God decreed and ensured they would commit this rebellion? I see no possible way. Why is He so angry over something He **planned** to happen!? Why would He put so many of these stories in the Bible if He wanted us to see only the God of Calvinism and their definition of sovereignty?

BUT, did God bring the Israelites into the land? Yes, He did. Was it according to plan A? No, it wasn't. But He worked plan B forty years later and made it happen anyway. He is not in a hurry. His will was not foiled. Is this the only time God adapted His plan? No, there are many. In fact, God is clear that He will do things He wouldn't have done because of us. In James 4:2, He says, "Ye have not because ye ask not." There is no hint that what they had or didn't have was because of some decree. This passage says you can change things with prayer. The onus was on them. Calvinists will say God decrees when or if I pray, and that its result is already predetermined; that prayer itself changes nothing.

Read Genesis 18 where Abraham bargains with God to spare Sodom and Gomorrah if a certain number of righteous people are found to be there. He starts at fifty. An interesting, and tender conversation then ensues in which Abraham, worried he might have under-negotiated, keeps adjusting the number until he gets to ten. God gives in to him. Did God want us to understand that, because He loves His children, He will actually change or adapt His plans to make them happy, just as an earthly Father often does?

Well, that would be the natural reading. Calvinists would state that God had already decreed what He was going to do. He had *decided* Abraham would engage in this negotiation, including every individual word he said, as well as any poor grammar used and every time he cleared his throat or blinked while doing it! According to them, Abraham changed nothing. This was a show. All the prayer promises essentially mean nothing.

John Piper uses the Cross as an example that God ordains murder to accomplish His will, without being the author of sin. The Cross could not have happened if He didn't "make" them kill His Son. Really? Is that the only way it could have happened? Did evil people have to be manipulated into killing His Son? Of course not. Evil people have been killing righteous people since Cain. Could God not use His foreknowledge to interweave His will in and around man's sin, to accomplish His will without *making them sin*? Well, according to them, no. It's apparently just too complicated. In the same way God cannot know the future without decreeing everything in the future, He cannot accomplish His will without making us sin. In spite of Genesis 18:14, I guess there are some things just too hard for Him to figure out. He is boxed in and can only work with what He has. The Calvinist God is *much weaker* and *more limited* than the God of free will. As one person said, He doesn't even seem sovereign over His sovereignty.

Note: Remember that people were crossing the line with Jesus and being hardened. They were being used as tools and pawns to accomplish His will just as Pharaoh was. They were being used as the vessels of wrath they now were to accomplish God's will.

Piper uses stories like that of Joseph, where God supposedly ordained the hate and sin of his brothers as an instrument to put Joseph in Egypt. Could God not have used His intimate knowledge of everyone's personal sin issues, logistics, and circumstances, to arrange His will a thousand different ways without *making* them sin? Of course He could. We don't have to understand how He does it. We *can't* understand how He does it. We just have to believe the clear teachings of His Word. God does not initiate sin! "Thou art of purer eyes than to behold evil, and canst not look on iniquity…" (Habakkuk 1:13) Oh, so He can't stand to *look* at sin, but He can make detailed plans about the dirty, evil, filthy, rotten things He is going to have His creatures do!? I don't think so! "Let no man say when he is tempted, I am tempted of God: for God cannot be tempted with evil, neither tempteth he any man. But every man is tempted, when he is drawn away of his *own* lust, and enticed."

Some Calvinists say God simply allows the circumstances knowing their motives will result in sin; so He is not to blame. If that were all they said, I wouldn't have a problem. But where did the *motives* of the heart come from? Did these lusts come from man? That's *impossible* according to them. They say **everything** comes from God and His decrees. He willed and made everything that is. These motives and lusts didn't happen apart from God. They had to come from Him! If Calvinists are right, this disgusting rot originates first in the mind of God; then He places it into people; then He places the opportunity to sin in front of them. He *makes* them sin! We already saw that with Adam.

The Calvinist definition of sovereignty is simply not the Bible definition. It is imagined, forced, and contrived. The Bible definition is seen over and over in the natural reading and interpretation God intended. He is sovereign while man simultaneously has truly free will. My personal theory is that Calvinists are so against free will because they don't see how it is possible for God *to even create* a separate being with its own actual independent will. I admit that is an amazing thing. I find it more astounding than His creating the stars. But I also believe God is up to the task. My theory extends to why they hate the idea of man having a choice in salvation. They simply don't believe the Spirit even *can* create a situation in His drawing where He enables the creature to make its own choice without making the choice Himself. Again, I believe my God can do it.

On a humorous note regarding sovereignty, I find it funny that Calvinists I have known looked for every chance to convert me to their side. Don't they realize that if they are right, God has already decided everything I'm going to do, say, feel, and believe? They don't need to work that hard! They can't make a difference anyway.

Before salvation, we are dead in sin. How can a dead person believe and receive Christ?

This harks back to the T in TULIP, which is Total Depravity. Although I mentioned I wouldn't be addressing it as a main item, it does warrant some delving into. You will find one of the major dividing lines between Calvinists and the free will camp stems from this question: **Does faith precede regeneration, or does regeneration precede faith?** Calvinists are compelled by their doctrine to state that God simply zaps someone into regeneration. They had nothing to do with it. They didn't think about it as a result of hearing the Gospel, they didn't become convicted of their sin and turn to God as a result, they didn't consider Jesus because of the testimonies of Christians. They were simply and suddenly just "saved" at a moment in time because God had decided they would be. Let's look at the Calvinist side and then the free will side.

Calvinists use the fact that we are spiritually dead, (what they call totally depraved), before salvation. How does a dead man respond to God? They use passages such as Ephesians 2:1, "And you hath he quickened, who were dead in trespasses and sins...", and Romans 3:10, 11, "As it is written, There is none righteous, no, not one: There is none that understandeth, there is none that seeketh after God.

I agree that none seek God on their own, but we've seen that the Holy Spirit draws people and does an enabling work when He offers salvation that one cannot do for himself. Why would He make useless offers that man cannot respond to? They use Philippians 1:29, "For unto you it is given in the behalf of Christ, not only to believe on him, but also to suffer for his sake." See there, it was "given" to us to believe, they say. I see no strength in this argument. God has given the offer of salvation to everyone. There is nothing here that negates the free will view.

They use John 3:3, "Except a man be born again, he cannot see the kingdom of God." Frankly, I don't see how they say this teaches regeneration precedes faith unless you just read that position into it. Maybe they are saying, "First he is regenerated, and only then can he see with the "eyes of faith?" I read it as simply saying if you don't become born again you will never see Heaven. What's wrong with the simple, natural reading? The Calvinist position is so weak on this point, though, that it seems they are grasping for any passage they can get.

They point to John 1:12, 13, "But as many as received him, to them gave he power to become the sons of God, even to them that believe on his name: which were born, not of blood, nor of the will of the flesh, nor of the will of man, but of God" to say that man's will is not part of salvation. I see no problem here. Man's will could never have saved him if God's will had not initiated a plan of salvation. Certainly, man cannot save himself simply with a decision to turn over a new leaf or to be righteous. It requires a supernatural work to be "born" spiritually; and only God can do that. Besides, look at the *first* part of the passage. He only made "sons of God" of the ones who **received** Him! He didn't suddenly make them sons, resulting in them "receiving" afterward, which wouldn't make any sense.

Calvinists quote I Corinthians 12:9 and Galatians 5:22 to say that since faith is a gift, we cannot produce it ourselves. We have to be regenerated *first*. That leads us to the fundamental difference between the two groups, that of how to understand faith as a gift. (We could say the same of repentance.) Calvinists understand the gift of faith to be a forcing of faith into a person against their will. God essentially believes for them. According to them, the gift of faith is *effectual*, meaning salvation is the inevitable result. For traditionalists, the gift of faith is the *enabling* of faith. That is, the lost person is able to choose to believe at the moment the Spirit is drawing, but is not deprived of his free will to make that choice.

We see Jesus rebuking lack of faith in Luke 9:41, "O faithless and perverse generation, how long shall I be with you, and suffer you?" In Luke 8:25, Jesus asks His disciples where their faith is. The disciples are already believers! He is rebuking people for not having faith when they should have. How much sense does it make to scold people for not having something only you can give them if you chose not to give it to them?!

This is the continual absurdity of Calvinism. God sends dead people to Hell for being dead, when He decided they would have no choice but to be dead! He blames them for not having faith, when only He can give it, and He decided not to give it! He makes them incapable of wanting Him, then tortures them for not wanting Him! Yet we are to accept that He is loving, good, merciful, and just! There is nothing scholarly or logical about Calvinism despite this general impression they have somehow managed to foist on the public. When you look behind the curtain, you see twisting, manipulation, shredded logic, and incoherence.

But, it makes perfect sense to rebuke people for not believing when they have been granted everything they need to believe—when they have been given the message and the enlightenment to understand it by the Holy Spirit. Romans 10:17 says faith comes by hearing the Word of God. It is not simply "zapped" into you. The Gospel itself is the power, Romans 1:16. It comes with the necessary supernatural enabling caused by the Spirit's drawing.

The term some traditionalists use is *prevenient grace*. That is the moment when God comes to a person and gives him an ability to make a decision he could not normally make. Calvinists say he is utterly dead! How does a dead person make a decision? Only God could. Well, that sounds reasonable if you are picturing a dead body. But when you remember that the *biblical* definition of death is separation from God, not a lifeless body lying on the floor, the picture changes. In the moment the Spirit is drawing that person, he is not separated. God is *there* with the individual, illuminating and making him or her see truth in a way they normally could not, giving what is needed to make a decision. Do I understand how it works? No, but my lack of understanding was never a barrier for God. I theorize that He is momentarily giving them the same ability of choice Adam and Eve had before the Fall; but it is only an idea. (By the "Fall," I'm talking about that of the free will view; not that of Calvinism where Adam was already unstable (evil) before he "fell.") In that case, logically there could not have been a "Fall."

Calvinists cannot produce a single text that **explicitly** requires us to understand that regeneration is the cause of faith. But traditionalists *can* produce passages that **do explicitly show** that faith is the cause of regeneration. (Keep in mind that faith and regeneration would, of course, happen in the same moment. There would be no delay. However, it is common to state that faith must happen first, because it is the condition for receiving regeneration.) Colossians 2:12 says that we are raised with Him *through* faith. I have seen Calvinists stumped and unable to explain this passage. There is simply no way to twist it to align with their doctrine and say God raised us first, then we believed.

Romans 4:3-5, Galatians 3:26, and James 2:23 teach clearly that Abraham first believed, then he was counted righteous. Well, you are only righteous because of being regenerated. Roman 5:1 says we are justified *by faith*. It had to come *first*. It is the cause. It is not the result of having first been justified. I Timothy 1:16 says we *believe* to *life everlasting*, not, that we have life everlasting to believe.

Jesus taught the Samaritan woman in John 10:10-14 that He must first be *asked* for the living water, then He *gives* the living water. You don't start out being alive and then ask for life! Jesus didn't start by zapping her alive. He required a *response from her first*! Luke 8:12 says the Devil takes the word out of people's hearts so that they will not *believe and be saved*. How could any of this possibly make sense if God simply instantaneously regenerates those He chooses to save.

The way the Gospel is preached in the Bible forces us to conclude that a decision precedes regeneration. If Calvinists are logically consistent with their own doctrine, then when asked what to do to be saved, they have to say, "There is nothing you can do. If God has chosen you, He will save you." There are those that actually do this! Fortunately, there are many that turn into freewillers for a moment, disregard their own doctrine, and actually urge people to make a decision and to receive Christ. This is the Bible way. When asked what to do in Acts 2:37, 38, Peter says, "Repent, and be baptized every one of you in the name of Jesus Christ for the remission of sins, and ye shall receive the gift of the Holy Ghost." Can it possibly be clearer that faith (evidenced by repentance) precedes regeneration? Try to make this passage say regeneration precedes faith. You can't do it! You can't do it with *any* of these passages!

When the Philippian jailer (Acts 16:30, 31) asked Paul, "What must I do to be saved?," he said, "Believe on the Lord Jesus Christ, and thou shalt be saved…" I challenge you to try to construct an explanation where the jailer was actually regenerated before he believed. If God had already saved him, he wouldn't have asked what to do to be saved; or Paul would have simply told him he was demonstrating that he was already saved and didn't need to do anything. Since he *wasn't* already saved, Paul should have known a "dead" person is not capable of hearing and responding to God until *after* he is save, and he shouldn't have even tried to give an invitation. He should have said, "There is nothing you can do. God will save you if He chooses."

I believe Calvinists have never thought this through, or they couldn't be Calvinists. If Calvinism is true, then if you are not saved, you cannot possibly ask for salvation. By the time you can actually ask for it, you already have it and don't need to ask for it! The invitation to believe and be saved becomes completely meaningless! Calvinists always say God uses *means*, even though He predestinates individuals to salvation. They concur that God chooses to save by the foolishness of preaching. (I Corinthians 1:21) But it makes no sense in a real situation.

In Acts 3:19, Peter again requires a decision first. He says, "Repent ye therefore, and be converted, that your sins may be blotted out…" *First comes faith*, which causes repentance. *Then the sins are blotted out* and reconciliation with God occurs.

Romans 10:9 says, "That if thou shalt confess with thy mouth the Lord Jesus, and shalt believe in thine heart that God hath raised him from the dead, thou shalt be saved." Ask yourself what is the order here. Did salvation come, and then faith as the result; or did faith precede regeneration? The truth is *explicit and inescapable*. The fact that faith precedes, and is the condition for regeneration, is one of the most basic, clear, and fundamental concepts of the Bible. Calvinists can never acknowledge this, as it would be the end of their doctrine. If there is a **condition** for man to be saved, it destroys their construct that God saves arbitrarily based on nothing man does, but only on His sovereign choice. It shows man has free will and must choose.

Is Calvinism really more scholarly than the traditional position? I submit it is not even close. It is nothing but a brazen twisting of scripture. Unfortunately and sadly, I have seen Calvinists tell people there is nothing they can do to be saved. Only God decides. *How many people are in Hell right now because they were told by a Calvinist they didn't have to do anything because they couldn't do anything?* This perversion of the Gospel has caused, and continues to cause, terrible and tragic harm. I have seen it drive people into atheism because of the contradictions between God's nature and actions in the Bible; or because they fear they are not elect. Derek Webb from Caedmon's Call is one of them.

What about the fact that we were chosen or predestinated?

These teachings are in the Bible and must be taken into account. So some investigation into what God meant us to learn is warranted. Ephesians 1:3-14, one of the Calvinist proof texts, teaches that we were chosen *in Him* (Christ) before the world began.

It is very important to understand that we have nothing at all that is not "in Christ." See 1:3 & 2:6; 1:4,6,7,11,13; 2:13; and 3:11,12. We were not chosen *to be placed in Christ*; it says we were "chosen in Christ" (1:4). This is a *vital* distinction, not only regarding the current topic, but the entire Christian life. Christ is the "Chosen One" according to Isaiah 42:1. Read it carefully. Why does it call Him "Chosen?" Were there several possible candidates for the position of Savior from whom Jesus was picked? Of course not. Clearly, it doesn't carry the normal sense here.

We are given a great clue in Matthew 12:18 where this same passage is quoted from Isaiah. Matthew, under the inspiration of the Holy Spirit substitutes the word "beloved" (agapetos) for the word "elect" (bachiyr) in the Hebrew. This close association between the state of electedness and belovedness is seen in other passages as well. In the Transfiguration account of Codex Sinaiticus, one of the most ancient Greek Bible texts, where the Father's voice is heard saying, "This is my beloved Son in whom I am well pleased, Matthew and Mark use the Greek word "agapetos" (beloved). But Luke cites the same account using the word "eklektos" (chosen). Another passage demonstrating this close association between belovedness and chosenness is I Peter 2:4-6.

So Christ is the Chosen or *Beloved* One, and we are chosen "in Him." We have no election of our own, but rather enter into His chosenness when we are saved. What is true of Him becomes true of us. We are chosen *in Him*. We are blessed and seated in the Heavenlies *in Him. His* death was our death. *His* resurrection is our resurrection. We enter God's presence, not alone, but always *in Him*. We are accepted *in* the Beloved One **only** (Eph. 1:6). So biblically, our chosenness is, not so much a case of eeny meeny miny mo, i.e. being picked at random out of a crowd, but of a state of belovedness which we received when we entered into Christ. We **become** elect by entering into the Elect One. When does this happen? Verse 13 is crystal clear. It happens *after*, and conditional upon, our *belief.* That is when the seal is bestowed! This is known as the *corporate view of election.* It was predestined, or foreordained, that this body would be holy and without blame in Christ.

Romans 8:29, 30 also teaches predestination. I believe this passage has been grossly misunderstood by both camps. The Calvinists, of course, say it teaches their version of unconditional predestination to salvation; and the traditionalists say it shows God looking through time and choosing whomever He saw would have a heart receptive to Him, which arguably, is a little weird, as the Calvinists love to point out.

What if there is another interpretation that is absolutely nothing like either camp is proposing, one that becomes visible if we take off the lenses of both sides and simply remember Paul's emphasis in Romans is God's dealings with the Jews and how the Gentiles are saved and benefited by them? I became aware of this view from reading Dr. Leighton Flowers, a former hardcore Calvinist, who left the doctrine after years of conflict between what he had been taught and what his own studies indicated. This book is meant to be a relatively brief study, but if you have the time, you can read his material and watch many hours of video refuting Calvinism. Simply Google his name and you will find these.

The word "foreknow" is "proginosko" in the Greek. It simply means to know before. The context is the key to determining if it means a prophetic knowing in advance, or simply knowing someone in time past. I agree with Dr. Flowers that here it is simply referencing the Old Testament saints God had a relationship with in the past.

First, notice that proginosko is used in this ordinary way in other places. In Acts 26:5, Paul, before Agrippa, refers to his accusers who knew him before when he was a Pharisee. The word he uses is proginosko. In II Peter 3:17, the apostle has given a warning, and says that since they now know these things ahead of time, using the word proginosko, they should not be caught unawares. Neither instance is referring to an ability to see through time.

Now please read Romans 8 and consider that Paul is speaking to people that are suffering for the cause of Christ (verse 17). He is making the case that, as God took care of His own in time past, He will also take care of them. The fact that he says, "We know" that God works all things for the good of His people is based specifically on the evidence we see in the Old Testament. He continues, saying that these saints He knew before, implying an intimate and loving relationship, He predestinated to be conformed to the image of His Son. They were given a calling, justified, and then glorified. Similarly, those who suffer for Christ today will ultimately end up the same way, glorified with Jesus.

Notice the past tense of the verbs in verses 29 and 30. That would be strange in light of the above-mentioned interpretations by both camps. The people they are talking about have not been glorified yet. They are in the future. Why not stay in the future tense as in verse 17? But if they are referring to completed action regarding the Jewish saints of old, the past tense not only makes sense; it is required.

This interpretation was held by theologians before, but seems to have somehow fallen to the wayside in the debates between the determinist and traditionalist views. It is not only a plausible interpretation; it seems to be the natural reading if you consider it. The traditionalist does not have to offer the Calvinist the weak view that God looked down through the corridors of time and, whenever He saw someone receptive, said, "I choose him/her!"

There is simply nothing in these passages fatal to the freewill view, or that erases the overwhelming scriptural evidence against *unconditional election, limited atonement,* and *irresistible grace* as taught by those holding the Calvinist position. I find it a *far* milder problem to blend these passages with the biblical teaching that God loves and wants to save everyone, than to attempt to explain away the multitude of passages clearly and purposefully teaching this.

Jesus said in John 15:16, "Ye have not chosen me but I have chosen you." A case can be made that since He was speaking only to the apostles at that time, He was referring to their *apostolic* election and ministry, not their salvation. We *must* interpret all Bible passages in light of how they fit with other passages.

If we say we made a decision to receive Christ, aren't we taking credit for part of our salvation?

Calvinists I have occasionally spoken with raise this issue, as if those emphasizing the free will of man think they had some part in their salvation if they assent that they *chose* to receive Him. For one thing, we've already seen that God tells us in numerous places *to make this choice*. So it is not wrong for me to say I received Him; that I made a decision. John 1:12 makes salvation contingent on *receiving* Jesus.

Secondly, if someone gave me a brand new car for free, and all I had to do was to decide to accept it, there would be no credit whatsoever on my part for being in possession of that car. No one would think I was taking any kudos for obtaining it simply because I told them I accepted it. The only reason we are in possession of salvation is because of the love, grace, and mercy of God. He did everything to provide it! We are taking zero credit for it by acknowledging we received it.

Conclusion:

Here I ask you to step back and look at the big picture. The Bible says "God IS love." It is His nature. Words mean something. They are to be interpreted logically and reasonably. The Calvinist God created the vast majority of human beings for the purpose of forcing them to sin, and then blaming them. He then burns them alive forever to make a show of His holiness and anger against the sin *He made happen* so He will get glory. He set aside a group of favorites who would see the fate of everyone else and love Him because He didn't do that to them. Does this sound like the God who *is* agape love to you, the One who exemplifies selflessness? Is this the God who delights in mercy and whose will is not to afflict any?

Calvinists would never state their doctrine this way because it highlights how horrible their God is. They are always choosing their words very carefully. In case you think I've stated the view too strongly, where is the inaccuracy? The fact is, if God decreed that man would sin because it was His will, then engineered everything so that man could not possibly have obeyed, *that is forcing*! Leaving no other possibility is *forcing!* There is no way to escape that conclusion except to abandon all logic and reason. *Burning them alive* is also reality. That is the definition of Hell; the fire of God's wrath and vengeance torturing the wicked. That is Bible. The devil didn't put them there; God did. In the judgment, His angels cast them there. Matthew 10:28 says to fear him that is able to destroy…in Hell. That is not the devil. He will be in ruin in Hell himself. It is speaking of God. Hebrews 10:31 says, "It is a fearful thing to fall into the hands of the living God." Hebrews 12:29 says, "Our God is a consuming fire."

The wicked who actually *did* choose wickedness over salvation brought that on themselves. It is just. It should be clear that is not what I'm referring to here. I'm referring to forcing man to sin, then burning him for it. There is *nothing* just about that. How could that possibly bring glory to God? How could that ever show *any* goodness and love?

I also use the word *show*. What else could you logically call a display of anger when it is regarding something He *wanted* to happen and *made* happen? The word *show* seems applicable to so many parts of this doctrine.

Calvinists constantly change the normal definitions of words to mean things that would never be applied to anything or anyone else. But somehow, that is just fine when talking about God or this doctrine.

> **Loving**: gracious to His favorites; hateful and fatal to all the rest
>
> **Good**: kind to His favorites but preferring to torture the rest, giving them no hope or alternative
>
> **All**: some; (actually, only a few)
>
> **Savior of the world**: one who makes salvation unavailable to the world, choosing instead to save a small subgroup
>
> **Choices of man**: choices of God
>
> **World**: the elect
>
> **Holiness of God**: His ability to engage in the unholy and simultaneously be holy
>
> **Justice**: eternal torture of people who were not allowed to do right but were blamed for it anyway
>
> **Justice** (alternate definition): punishment of people who engage in the unholy by a God who also engages in the unholy
>
> **Hero**: one who places others in peril so he can save them and get glory
>
> **Wrath of God**: show of "anger" over what He actually wanted, and forced to happen
>
> **Fatherhood**: a "relationship" where the father decides and preprograms everything the child thinks, does, says, or feels

Judgment Seat: rewards or loss awarded to Christians for the things God alone decided they would do

John Wesley, preaching with great anger against Calvinism, called it blasphemy, and stated it destroys the attributes of God: love, compassion, mercy, and justice. If what Calvinism says is true, you can stand on the corner of a crowded street and watch thousands of people; and you will have to conclude that God doesn't care about most of them. Most have no hope. Is this a loving God? Would you call someone who turns a flamethrower on everyone except his or her friends loving? Of course not. The definition of a loving person is someone who treats *everyone* with compassion. Words mean something or they are worthless. Jesus promised to draw "all men" in John 12:32. Just because it looks like He is not drawing some doesn't mean He didn't. Just because He hasn't given the same amount of light to everyone doesn't mean He didn't draw them. In the Old Testament, He gave even Gentiles the option to be saved, and many were. They didn't have the same amount of light, but salvation was still for them. Israel was the witness through whom God showed Himself to them because His plan was for them to know of Him and come to Him. (I Kings 8:41-43; I Samuel 17:46; II Kings 19:19; Psalm 67:1-4)

I consider Calvinism heresy and an abomination. At the same time I consider Calvinists themselves to be Christians and sincere servants of Christ, who have been led astray. Many are soulwinners, and are actively serving Him the best they know how. All indications are that the men I mentioned by name in this treatise are good, intelligent people, men of integrity, and genuine Christians who love God. Nothing was meant to be an attack on their person; only their truly horrific doctrine. I used their names because they have already placed themselves in the public eye; and I want you to be able to examine their teachings for yourself so that I am not the only representation you see.

I consider it one of the great tragedies of history that Calvin ever wrote the things he did and steered so many people down the wrong road. The Catholic Augustine had similar ideas in the fifth century, but the doctrine was not at all prominent before Calvin. It was not the general doctrine of the Christian Church Fathers, and was not even propounded before Augustine according to Calvinist Lorraine Boettner. If it is such a *vital* "truth," how did *most* of God's people survive *most* of the Church Age without it? That alone should make it quite suspect. Its sudden materialization is reminiscent to me of a cult.

No matter what view of election you take, you will encounter verses in Scripture that *seem* to contradict. This is a simple fact. I believe God provided salvation for all, because I find the associated hermeneutical problems to be extremely mild relative to those of the antithetical view. I have rejected Calvinism because, after extensive study of the issue, I have concluded that *unconditional election, limited atonement,* and *irresistible grace,* not only encounter impossible contradictions with a multitude of scriptural passages, but also present serious problems when examining the overall cohesion and purpose of the Bible.

Jehovah's Witnesses are not without their proof texts; and Calvinists are not without theirs. They appeal to scripture to arrive at their positions. But they have almost entirely ignored, redefined, or manipulated a huge number of passages of Scripture so as not to embrace their natural reading. Their doctrine, to me, is like a Picasso painting. Everything is twisted, distorted, unnatural, and ugly. Up is down, and down is up. Good is evil, and evil is good. God forced sin on the world, but He is not the author of sin. He engages in the unholy but sends people to Hell for engaging in the unholy. The One who IS love lights most of His creatures on fire to get glory. He is bound by time and cannot figure out how to be sovereign unless He controls all movement and thought. He is, essentially, the great *contriver*. Nothing is genuine. Everything is rigged. The Word becomes a mess of hopeless contradiction. It is not a message of hope to the world; it is a message of pure horror regarding most and cause for great sighs of relief from the lucky few who won the drawing and escaped. Calvinists insist that God chose with great purpose whom to save. At the same time, they maintain His choices had nothing whatsoever to do with any characteristics in the elect. What does that leave but arbitrary choice? —eeny meeny miny mo. It was, essentially, the great *lottery*. Who will burn and who won't. This is truly a doctrine of the devil; and its god is just as evil. It is a terrible tragedy that such great blasphemy against the *true* God was introduced into His family. Many Christians suffer from depression and stress because of the horror and contradictions in God's attributes and actions they are taught. I have seen people struggle with fear because they are afraid they are not really elect. Some have gone into atheism because nothing makes sense.

Calvinist teachings can have very negative consequences in the church, especially among newer Christians who haven't conditioned themselves to be hard and resilient. If they think their efforts in God's service are ultimately ineffective, that everything is already fixed, and that the only reason we are in this battle is to receive a blessing, not to make a difference in the destination of souls; how will they be excited and motivated for ministry like they would be if they knew their work, prayers, and testimonies make a genuine difference?

What of the teaching that God decrees all of your sins? What is the motivation to the Christian to resist temptation? If you succumb, it is because God chose for you to succumb. You can tell yourself there was nothing else you could do, that God is responsible, not you.

According to Calvinism, you can choose to go out right now and do anything you happen to feel like; and whatever you do, God preordained and decreed it because He wanted it to happen. Calvinists would never say this, but it is the only possible conclusion since they maintain nothing can happen except what God has deliberately willed and predetermined.

I feel badly for all new Christians sitting in pews listening to this rot because they don't know any better. Fortunately, there are those who think for themselves instead of blindly accepting what a preacher says. Many have eventually come out of Calvinism after seeing the blatant contradictions and inconsistencies. Sadly, most never think for themselves, and stay in it permanently.

This doctrine, although against the will of its adherents, detracts from the glory of God and destroys His reputation. He is seen as a Being who gives no hope to most people, choosing to torture them out of preference. This causes Him to be perceived as a monster, and rightly so. The Calvinist God sacrifices His creatures for Himself. The true God sacrificed Himself for His creatures. The Calvinist God is the most selfish being in the universe. The true God is the most selfless.

In my opinion, the true God gets much greater glory from His amazing and genuine grace to all. He has emphasized time and again in His Word that He loves with a love that is beyond our understanding, that His grace is greater than our sin, that He delights in mercy, and that He wants all to be saved. For this, we will praise Him for all eternity!

This doctrine can also promote an "us-and-them" mentality. "We are the elect. They are not." "God loves us. He doesn't love them." But we need to empathize with all the lost, constantly bearing in mind that we are not better than they, but were simply hopeless sinners as well, upon whom others of the redeemed had compassion, telling us about a Savior who not only rescued them, but offers His precious gift to all.

Again, this work was not intended to be a comprehensive refutation of all points of Calvinism nor an exhaustive study on election. Instead, the purpose was to dwell on certain sub points that I believe *can* be exegeted with a high degree of certainty. Biblically, I don't believe there can be any question that Jesus loves and purchased salvation for all, that it is truly available to all, and that His grace can be resisted and rejected by man.

Reader, I urge you to evaluate this doctrine for yourself. Don't be a sheep, accepting the words of a Bible teacher just because they may seem to sound good. Be a true student of the Word and prayerfully let God guide you in your doctrine. This book is one of many study aids. It is not a substitute for the Holy Spirit, although my prayer is that it may be a tool in His hands. May God bless and guide you as you continue to study His Word.

Here is a brief topical list of passages against each tenet, although there are plenty more if you wish to add to it on your own. Some of them are used more than once. Notice the tenets are intertwined. Unconditional Election leads naturally to Limited Atonement. Why would Jesus die for those He did not intend to save? Unconditional Election necessitates Irresistible Grace. If God picked them out, then He must save them by force. The three stand or fall together, and therefore, each passage against one is ultimately a passage against all.

Unconditional Election
Deuteronomy 5:29; 32:29; Proverbs 23:13,14; Lamentations 3:33; Ezekiel 18:4-32; 33:11; Matthew 9:36; 19:23,24; 23:13-15; Luke 13:34; John 1:7-9; 3:16; 4:42; 6:33; 12:32; Acts 10:34,35; Romans 5:18; 11:32; Titus 2:11; I Timothy 2:4; II Peter 3:9; I John 4:7,8

Limited Atonement
John 1:29; 4:42; 12:32; Acts 10:34,35; Romans 5:18; 11:32; II Corinthians 5:14,15; Colossians 1:19,20; I Timothy 4:10; Hebrews 2:9; I John 2:2; 4:14; II Peter 2:1

Irresistible Grace
Gen. 6:3-7; Deuteronomy 5:29; 32:29; Isa. 63:8-10; Ezekiel 18:30-32; 33:11; Mat. 23:37; John 5:40; Eph. 4:30; I Thessalonians 5:19; I Timothy 2:4; Titus 2:11; II Peter 3:9

Printed in Great Britain
by Amazon

86623873R00058